TWAYNE'S WORLD AUTHORS SERIES

A Survey of the World's Literature

Sylvia E. Bowman, Indiana University

GENERAL EDITOR

AUSTRIA

Ulrich Weisstein, Indiana University

EDITOR

SIGMUND FREUD

TWAS 357

SIGMUND FREUD

Sigmund Freud

By GERALD LEVIN

University of Akron

TWAYNE PUBLISHERS

A DIVISION OF G. K. HALL & CO., BOSTON

Library of Congress Cataloging in Publication Data

Levin, Gerald Henry, 1929-
  Sigmund Freud.

  (Twayne's world authors series; TWAS 357: Austria)
  Bibliography: pp. 161-67.
  Includes index.
  1. Freud, Sigmund, 1856-1939. 2. Psychoanalysis
BF173.F85L397   150'.19'52   74-31135
ISBN 0-8057-2330-7

To my mother and father

Contents

About the Author

Gerald Levin was born in Chicago, Illinois in 1929; he studied at the University of Chicago (M.A., 1952) and the University of Michigan (Ph.D., 1956). He was a pre-doctoral instructor at Michigan and later taught at the University of Colorado and Eastern Illinois University. He is now Professor of English at the University of Akron, where he has been teaching since 1960. His publications include articles on Conrad, Yeats, Lawrence, Shaw, Ruskin, Swinburne, Ford Madox Ford and Samuel Richardson, in a number of journals including *Literature and Psychology*, *Nineteenth-Century Fiction*, *American Imago*, *Journal of Modern Literature* and *Philological Quarterly*. He is the author of *Prose Models* (Third Edition, 1975), *A Brief Handbook of Rhetoric* (1966), *The Short Story* (1967), and *Styles for Writing* (1971); he is the co-author with Francis Connolly of *The Rhetoric Case Book*, Third Edition (1969); he completed and edited Francis Connolly's *The Art of Rhetoric* (1968).

Preface

No great modern scientist has exhibited a greater range of literary interest, a greater knowledge of ancient and modern literature, than Sigmund Freud. He knew Latin and Ancient Greek; in addition to his native German, he wrote and spoke English, French, Italian, and Spanish. Sophocles, Shakespeare, Dante, Cervantes, Flaubert, Ibsen, Goethe, Dostoevsky—to name only a few of the writers he knew well—made deep impressions on his life and work. Though his reading in philosophy was occasional and unsystematic, his thinking on traditional issues of philosophy was wide-ranging and profound; in later years he read Schopenhauer and Nietzsche, seeking corroboration for his theory of the Death Instinct.

These interests shaped Freud the writer as well as Freud the scientist, joining the language of empirical observation with that of philosophical discourse, in the manner of John Stuart Mill, some of whose essays he translated into German as a young man. In the words of Thomas Mann, Freud developed into an "artist of thought."[1]

A discernible pattern emerges in his writings over six decades. Stated in the broadest terms, his early writings are experimental and inductive; his middle and late writings deductive and increasingly speculative, though grounded in and supported by observation and clinical experience. Brilliant and sometimes isolated insights and strands of thought eventually became part of an immense and richly elaborated structure of thought; nothing was wasted. I shall try to show that this is particularly true of Freud's theory of art and literature, which more than one commentator has dismissed as occasional and incoherent.

I shall also try to show that these ideas gave form to a highly tragic sense of life that guided Freud's thinking as a scientist and shaped his literary style. Philip Rieff suggests that Freud was the heir of the Stoic tradition that assumes the passions to be mysterious and autonomous.[2] Defining the instincts as "psychic representatives" or the mental equivalents of bodily feelings, Freud was able to conceive of them as forces of nature corresponding to inner drives, and he increasingly stressed their mysteriousness. Having begun with pathological man and with singular neurosis, he thought his way to man plural and universal. Increasingly his theme is the classic theme of freedom and necessity as experienced by all men. Life itself is pathological; his hero is the fully conscious individual, perpetually divided, and accepting his living and dying as wholly self-willed. Freud sustained this view of the irresolution of feeling in his final and controversial dual theory of the life and death instincts, in which his tragic view of man is finally posited. John Wren-Lewis has stated the philosophical impulse or disposition that shaped this view of man:

The discovery that men's ideas of gods, demons, angels and other metaphysical principles are projections of inner fantasies undoubtedly dispels a delusion, but to call it a delusion of grandeur [as Freud did] is to take over, consciously or unconsciously, religion's own valuation of inner feelings and fantasies as worthless in their own right, meaningful only in so far as they are believed to reflect a spiritual universe outside the individual human psyche.[3]

Though trained in the materialist view of man, and holding all his life to the view that psychological phenomena are grounded in physiological processes, Freud sought to free his thinking from limiting assumptions and to enlarge his frame of discourse. The increasing flexibility of his language was an important means to this end. Contrary to the popular view that he was authoritarian and dogmatic, he was quick to alter his position on major issues when he saw the necessity to do so, even when he found himself skirting ideas he had fought about with former colleagues like Adler and Jung. There is considerable evidence that he regarded his major formulations as hypotheses and clearly recognized the semantic problems his critics have dwelt on. In the opinion of one commentator (who argues that Freud's thinking was mainly physicalist), his strength as a scientist was precisely his willingness to let the contradictions of his thought stand.[4]

My concern in this study of Freud as a writer is chiefly with his characteristic mode of thought as it evolved over a lifetime and increasingly shaped a structure of ideas. I have not attempted to deal with Freud's characteristic German phrasing and style; the discussion throughout is based on the English translations of the Standard Edition, to which the citations in the text refer, and is limited accordingly. I have omitted from consideration writings of the pre-psychoanalytic period, the highly technical papers on analytic technique and the psychoneuroses, and most of the popular and encyclopedic expositions. I have given an account of and discussed the major writings and all the essays that bear on Freud's theory of art and literature or have intrinsic literary value.

Acknowledgments

Acknowledgment is made to the following publishers for permission to quote from the works listed:

The Hogarth Press Ltd., Sigmund Freud Copyrights Ltd., and The Institute of Psycho-Analysis, for permission to quote from *The Standard Edition of the Complete Psychological Works of Sigmund Freud*, revised and edited by James Strachey.
The Hogarth Press Ltd. and Basic Books, Inc., Publishers. From Letters 26, 28 and 153 of *The Letters of Sigmund Freud*, selected and edited by Ernst L. Freud, translated by James and Tania Stern, © 1960 Sigmund Freud Copyrights Ltd., London; Basic Books, Inc., Publishers, New York.

Basic Books, Inc., Publishers. From *Collected Papers of Sigmund Freud*, Volumes I, II and IV, edited by Ernest Jones, M. D., authorized translation under the supervision of Joan Riviere; Volume III, authorized translation by Alix and James Strachey; Volume V, edited by Ernest Jones, M. D., and edited by James Strachey, published by Basic Books, Inc., by arrangement with The Hogarth Press and The Institute of Psycho-Analysis, London.

From *Studies on Hysteria*, by Josef Breuer and Sigmund Freud, translated from the German and edited by James Strachey in collaboration with Anna Freud, assisted by Alix Strachey and Alan Tyson, published in the United States by Basic Books, Inc., by arrangement with The Hogarth Press Ltd.

W. W. Norton and Company, Inc. From *The Ego and the Id*, translated by Joan Riviere; revised and newly edited by James Strachey, 1960. *Civilization and its Discontents*, translated by James Strachey, 1961. *New Introductory Lectures on*

Psychoanalysis, newly translated and edited by James Strachey, 1965. *Psychopathology of Everyday Life*, translated by Alan Tyson and edited by James Strachey, 1966. *Jokes and Their Relation to the Unconscious*, newly translated and edited by James Strachey, 1960. *Leonardo da Vinci and a Memory of His Childhood*, translated by Alan Tyson, 1964, *Totem and Taboo*, authorized translation by James Strachey, 1950. *An Autobiographical Study*, authorized translation by James Strachey, 1963. *An Outline of Psychoanalysis*, translated and newly edited by James Strachey, 1969. *The Question of Lay Analysis*, translated and edited by James Strachey, 1969.

Liveright Publishers: From *Introductory Lectures on Psychoanalysis, Beyond the Pleasure Principle, Group Psychology and the Analysis of the Ego*, and *The Future of an Illusion*.

Routledge and Kegan Paul Ltd. From *Jokes and Their Relation to the Unconscious, Leonardo da Vinci* and *Totem and Taboo*.

George Allen and Unwin Ltd. From *Introductory Lectures on Psychoanalysis*.

Alfred A. Knopf, Inc. From *Moses and Monotheism* by Sigmund Freud, translated by Katherine Jones. Copyright 1939.

Chronology

1856	Sigmund Freud born May 6, Freiburg, Moravia.
1859	Moves with family to Leipzig and, a year later, to Vienna, living for a time in the Jewish quarter.
1865	Enters Sperl Gymnasium by examination a year before the usual age.
1873	Graduates *summa cum laude*; enters the University of Vienna to study medicine; studies physiology with Ernst Brücke.
1875	Journey to England, visiting his half-brothers Emanuel and Philipp in Manchester.
1876	Engages in research on evolutionary and neurological structures at experimental laboratory in Trieste and later at Brücke's institute; leading to a discovery in the histology of the spinal cord of the Amoecetes genus of fish.
1881	Becomes a doctor of medicine in March; Demonstrator in Brücke's institute; deepening friendship with Josef Breuer.
1882	Enrolls in General Hospital of Vienna in July, specializing in surgery; enters Nothnagel's Clinic as Aspirant in October; engagement to Martha Bernays.
1883	Psychiatric service at Meynert's Psychiatric Clinic at the hospital for five months (May 1); beginning October 1 serves in the Department of Dermatology.
1884	Experimentation with cocaine as an anesthetic; serves in Department of Nervous Diseases.
1885	Serves in Department of Ophthalmology (March 1); *Privatdozent* (Lecturer) in Neuropathology (September 5); studies in Paris, in the fall and winter of

	1885–86, at Hôpital de la Salpêtrière under Charcot; leaves hospital at end of August.
1886	Marries Martha Bernays on September 13; opens private medical practice (April 25).
1887	Birth of daughter, Mathilde; meets Fliess through Breuer; use of hypnosis in treating patients.
1889	Birth of son, Martin.
1891	Birth of son, Oliver; move to 19 Berggasse, Freud's home until 1938; book on aphasia; monograph on paralysis in children.
1892	Birth of son, Ernst.
1893	Birth of daughter, Sophie; monographs on paralysis in children.
1894	Cooling of friendship with Breuer.
1895	*Studies on Hysteria*, written with Breuer; birth of daughter, Anna; first visit to Italy (many visits in later years).
1896	Death of Jakob Freud in October.
1897	Freud's self-analysis.
1898	First public statement of theory of infantile sexuality.
1899	First of many family vacations at Berchtesgaden; writing and publication (November 4) of *The Interpretation of Dreams*.
1900	Course of lectures at University of Vienna; last meeting with Fliess.
1901	First visit to Rome.
1902	Formation of Psychological Wednesday Society (Freud, Kahane, Reitler, Stekel, Adler); end of correspondence with Fliess.
1904	*Psychopathology of Everyday Life*; visit to Greece; correspondence with Eugen Bleuler, leading Zurich psychiatrist and associate of Jung.
1905	*Jokes and Their Relation to the Unconscious; Three Essays on the Theory of Sexuality*.
1906	Beginning of correspondence with Jung; first meeting with Rank.
1907	First meeting with Jung, Abraham, Ferenczi, Eitington.
1908	Formation of Vienna Psychoanalytical Society; first

international conference in Salzburg; visit to England and Holland.

1909   Visit to United States, with Ferenczi and Jung; lectures and reception of honorary doctorate at Clark University; founding of *Jahrbuch der Psychoanalyse*, edited by Jung.

1910   Second international conference in Nuremberg (later conferences in 1911 and 1913); *Leonardo da Vinci*; founding of *Zentralblatt für Psychoanalyse*, edited by Adler and Stekel.

1911   Rupture with Adler; founding of *Imago*; founding of American Psychoanalytic Association.

1912   Rupture with Stekel; formation of the "Committee"; founding of *Zeitschrift für Psychoanalyse*.

1913   Rupture with Jung; founding of London association; *Totem and Taboo*.

1914   Jung leaves the International Association.

1915   Essays on metapsychology.

1915-
1916   *Introductory Lectures in Psychoanalysis*, the last of Freud's lectures at the University of Vienna.

1918   Budapest conference.

1919   Founding of psychoanalytic publishing house, Internationaler Psychoanalytischer Verlag; appointment as full professor in the University of Vienna, without faculty status or teaching duties.

1920   Hague conference (psychoanalytic conferences in later years); death of daughter Sophie; founding of *International Journal of Psychoanalysis; Beyond the Pleasure Principle*.

1921   *Group Psychology and the Analysis of the Ego*.

1923   *The Ego and the Id*; first of many operations for cancer of the jaw.

1924   Beginning of *Gesammelte Schriften*; rupture with Rank.

1925   *Autobiographical Study*; death of Breuer and Abraham.

1926   *Inhibitions, Symptoms and Anxiety; The Question of Lay Analysis*; meeting with Einstein.

1927   *The Future of an Illusion*; "Committee" ceases existence.

1929	Cooling of friendship with Ferenczi.
1930	*Civilization and Its Discontents*; receives Goethe Prize; death of mother.
1933	Burning of Freud's books in Germany; *New Introductory Lectures*; death of Ferenczi.
1936	Corresponding Member of Royal Society.
1938	Germans enter Vienna; Freud's house invaded by the S. A. and later by the Gestapo; departure from Austria, June 4; journey through France to England, settling finally in London; *Moses and Monotheism*; final operation for cancer.
1939	Death, September 23.
1940	*Outline of Psychoanalysis*; beginning of publication of *Gesammelte Werke*.

CHAPTER 1

The Life and Times of Sigmund Freud

I Education and Early Professional Life

S IGMUND Freud was born on May 6, 1856, in Freiburg, Moravia (now a part of Czechoslovakia). He believed that his father Jakob was descended from Cologne Jews who in the late Middle Ages fled east to escape anti-Semitism. His mother, Amalie, was from southeastern Poland and had lived in Odessa and Vienna as a child. Freud was the eldest son of a second marriage; he had two step-brothers, who were more than twenty years older than he and eventually settled in England, two brothers (one dying in infancy), and five sisters. His wool business increasingly threatened by anti-Semitism, the father moved the family first to Leipzig in 1859, and then in 1860 to Vienna, where they settled.[1]

Jakob Freud read the Torah and probably sent Sigmund to the synagogue for occasional instruction. The family observed the Passover, but other holidays and the dietary laws seem to have been neglected. Christmas and the Gentile New Year were routinely observed.[2] These details and others have often been cited as evidence that Freud grew up in a "freethinking" atmosphere; but possibly, as in Jewish and Gentile households today, where religious holidays are observed even though traditional ways have lapsed, the attitude was one of indifference to religion.

All that can be said with certainty is that, though he professed himself an atheist, all his life Freud identified with Jewish cultural ideals and values. "We preserved our unity through ideas," he wrote in 1938, "and because of them we have survived to this day." He told Ernest Jones that the Jews had developed their brains one-sidedly, and on another occasion that he often identified with his passionate ancestors who had defended the Temple, and that like them he could sacrifice his life for a noble cause. He wrote the Vienna B'nai B'rith on his seventieth birthday: "Because I was a Jew I found myself free from many prejudices which restricted others in the use of their intellect; and as a Jew I was prepared to join the Opposition and to do without agreement with the 'compact majority.' "[3]

Friedrich Heer suggests that Freud's decision in 1879 to change his name Sigismund (the popular Jewish name in anti-Semitic jokes) was "a subconscious withdrawal from his own Jewishness."[4] That motive seems at odds with the fierce pride he exhibited all his life. He was not only the eldest son but the favorite child, and the only one to have his own room; and as he stated in *The Interpretation of Dreams*, the favorites of the mother "give evidence in their lives of a peculiar self-reliance and an unshakeable optimism which often seem like heroic attributes and bring actual success to their possessors" (V, 398). His boyhood heroes included Hannibal and Alexander the Great. He identified also with the Biblical Joseph and Moses; and later in life he came to admire Voltaire, Kant, and Darwin—thinkers who stood against the "compact majority." His often-quoted statement that his father had acquitted himself badly in an anti-Semitic street incident, if true, probably explains why Freud was aggressive in such encounters in his own life.[5]

His father taught him until the age of nine, at which time Freud entered the Sperl Gymnasium by examination a year early. He graduated *summa cum laude* in 1873, and in the fall entered the University of Vienna, taking work in the sciences. Almost immediately, he felt himself in an environment hostile to Jews (XX, 9).

In 1876 he began a series of research projects, first at an experimental laboratory in Trieste under his teacher in zoology, the eminent evolutionist Carl Claus, and in the Institute of Physiology in Vienna under another teacher, Ernst Brücke. Perhaps for the first time Freud felt that his talents were being well used.

During those years he made important contributions to evolution-ary theory; according to Jones, he anticipated the neurone theory; and in experiments with cocaine, he anticipated its use as an anesthetic. Following his appointment as a medical doctor in 1881, he left the Institute and in July of the following year en-tered the General Hospital of Vienna, specializing in surgery. In October he entered Nothnagel's Division of Internal Medicine as an assistant. In his three years at the hospital he devoted himself to dermatology, ophthalmology, and nervous diseases and gained experience in Meynert's Psychiatric Clinic.

Freud's medical service at the hospital ended on August 31, 1885; on September 5 he was appointed a lecturer in neuropathology at the university (he was honored as "professor" by the Emperor in 1902 and was appointed full professor in 1919, but without faculty status or teaching responsibilities). Later in 1885 he travelled to Paris, where for seventeen weeks he studied hypnosis, neurology, and psychology with the great Charcot.

The impact of Charcot's personality and scientific skill on Freud was enormous, in particular his attention to the least noticeable qualities of mental life. Charcot "had the nature of an artist," he wrote in 1893; he was a "*visuel*, a man who sees" (III, 12). Returning to Vienna, he performed his last experiments, though he continued to write on neurology (he published a book on aphasia in 1891). Henceforth he devoted himself to psychopathology.

In October of 1886, he read a paper on Charcot's work with male hysterics before the Vienna Society of Physicians. According to Freud, his statements were dismissed as unbelievable, and his former teacher, the influential Meynert, challenged him to prove his claims. That, however, became impossible, for he was soon afterwards excluded from Meynert's laboratory, as well as from work with other physicians in the hospital (XX, 15–16). Earlier that year he had opened a private medical practice, mainly treat-ing nervous ailments with electrotherapy and later hypnosis (for a period of eighteen months, beginning in December, 1887). In April, 1896, he read a paper on the causes of hysteria at a meet-ing of a Vienna psychiatric association chaired by Krafft-Ebing.. "The donkeys gave it an icy reception," he wrote Fliess after-wards (III, 189). The general disapproval of his ideas seems to have discouraged active professional associations; the ten-year period which Freud dated from his break with his colleague Joseph Breuer in 1894 he regarded as one of "splendid isolation."

II *Marriage and Friendship*

Freud became engaged to Martha Bernays in June, 1882, and married her in September, 1886. Martha was five years younger than he; she came from Hamburg, where her grandfather (related to Heine) had been the chief rabbi and a leader in the Jewish Reform movement; her brother Eli married Freud's oldest sister in 1883. Between 1887 and 1895 she bore six children—three sons and three daughters. In 1896 her sister Minna joined the household, eventually forming a close intellectual relationship with Freud.

Freud wrote Martha more than nine hundred letters during the years of betrothal. Those published are among the greatest in world literature. The first impression they give is of a directness of expression, ardor, and total absorption suggestive of Mozart, but without his spontaneity and playfulness. Freud discusses at length Martha's qualities of mind and the effect his character would have upon her. He is a man who knows he will have his way:

As far as my activities allow we shall read together what we want to learn, and I will initiate you into things which could not interest a girl so long as she is unfamiliar with her future companion and his occupation. All that has happened and is happening will, by the interest you take in it, become an added interest for me. You will not judge me according to the success I do or do not achieve, but according to my intentions and my honesty; you will not regret having sacrificed the beautiful years of your youth to fidelity, and I shall be proud of you.[6]

Preserving her purity of mind is a dominant concern; *Don Quixote* is improper reading for his "lovely princess"; and he worries about "coarse" and "nauseating passages" in the literature he sent to her. He is certain about the role fitted for the woman in life:

It seems a completely unrealistic notion to send women into the struggle for existence in the same way as men. Am I to think of my delicate sweet girl as a competitor? After all, the encounter could only end by my telling her, as I did seventeen months ago, that I love her, and that I will make every effort to get her out of the competitive role into the quiet, undisturbed activity of my home. It is possible that a different education could suppress all women's delicate qualities—which are so much in need of protection and yet so powerful—with the result that they could earn their living like men. It is also possible that in this case it would not be justifiable to deplore the disappearance of the most lovely thing the world has to offer us: our ideal of womanhood. (November 15, 1883)

The following letter to his daughter Sophie in 1912, occasioned by her sudden engagement to a man Freud had not met, shows that Freud never lost the touch of mixing sternness with affection so that, to paraphrase a character of Dickens, discipline is maintained:

Another father in my situation would write that he cannot understand how a telegram saying "Mama Papa Max congratulate you" could possibly be construed in any other sense than: We congratulate you on your engagement, greet you as a bride—and he wouldn't be able to understand how such a greeting could possibly produce dissatisfaction. I, however, can imagine that you are somewhat bothered by your conscience for having ignored us so completely when you decided to get engaged, and this at least is to your credit. The degree of your remorse may be judged by the fact that you even succeeded in upsetting your Aunt, normally so imperturbable. (July 20, 1912)

Though the ardor of his first years of marriage seems to have waned, as he became absorbed in work and friendship, his relationship to his family remained unusually intimate and free of conflict. His son Martin states: "I do not think there were many children of middle-class parents at that time who enjoyed the freedom we enjoyed or accepted quite naturally the trust shown in us by our parents."[7]

The friendship that first absorbed him was with the physician Joseph Breuer, whom he met in the late 'seventies. The second important friendship was with the Berlin physician Wilhelm Fliess, whom he met through Breuer in 1887. With the exaggeration of which he was capable, he praised Fliess as the "Kepler of biology" for theories relating to menstruation and the rhythm of the universe, and he later credited Fliess with the theory of bisexuality. Jones suggests that Freud was attracted to his mercurial, self-confident manner, particularly to his imaginative leap to generalizations. He suggests also that the relationship was intellectually retarding since it tied Freud to physiological explanations longer than would have been the case had he not known Fliess. Their meetings ended in 1900, their correspondence in 1902, following a cooling of the friendship. Freud's view was that a feminine side of him demanded an intimate friendship and years later referred to "some piece of unruly homosexual feeling," in a comment to Jones.

The period of these friendships—coinciding with the period of professional isolation and his most original and daring thinking (fortunately preserved in his letters to Fliess)—was one of severe psychoneurosis and "hypochondriacal depression" for Freud.[8] Perhaps his father's death in October, 1896 impelled him to undertake his own analysis in the following summer. The extensive correspondence with Fliess was no doubt a seeking of the indispensable listener. The experience, the letters testify, was one of discovery and wonderment at the outcome. "I believe I am in a cocoon, and heaven knows what sort of creature will emerge from it," he wrote Fliess in December, 1897.[9] It is remarkable that he was able to conduct his analysis by devoting the last half hour of an exhausting day to it.

III   Vienna Before World War I

The milieu in which Freud developed as a man and scientist deserves brief comment. It is usual to state that Vienna served as a negative influence on Freud, providing opposition to his qualities of mind. The evidence is contradictory. He may have disliked the spirit of the city, characterized by Frederick Hacker in these words: "Being and appearing, reality and fancy imperceptibly merged into each other to produce the durable Viennese mixture of lightheaded muddling-through, of elastic inflexibility and gay melancholy."[10] Nevertheless Freud refused to leave the city until the Nazis forced him into exile, though he had numerous opportunities to establish a practice elsewhere.

It is usually pointed out that Vienna was one of the most anti-Semitic cities of Europe. The openly anti-Semitic Christian Social Party flourished toward the end of the nineteenth century under

Karl Lueger (revered by Hitler), who became Burgomaster in 1895 and immediately began to vilify the Jews. This situation, however, was not extraordinary. Jews in these years suffered persecution in many European countries, especially in Russia and Germany where anti-Semitic political parties and unions flourished. The condition of the Jews of Austria was materially better than in other countries, though the poverty of the Jewish quarter of Vienna was notorious.

Indeed, compared to the situation in Russia, the Jews of Vienna flourished, comprising twelve percent of the population in 1890 (in Germany in the 1880's, they comprised less than two percent). Undoubtedly the emphasis on education in Jewish life contributed to their relative prosperity. At least a third of the students at the University of Vienna in the 1890's, nearly half the faculty of medicine, almost a quarter of the faculty of law, and about fifteen percent of the faculty of philosophy, and most of the physicians of the city were Jewish.[11] Many of these Jews, like Freud, had become assimilated into the culture of the city, more so than other immigrant people who were not German speaking. Many, like Arthur Schnitzler, Ludwig Wittgenstein, Gustav Mahler, and Arnold Schoenberg, exerted a strong influence on cultural life and were to influence the course of European thought and culture in the twentieth century; some of these men, like Mahler and Schoenberg, lost sight of, or turned away from, Judaism and Jewish culture altogether. (Schoenberg made a significant return in the 1930's, the period of his great liturgical and Biblically inspired works which extended to his death in 1951.) Many were conservative in politics and anti-Zionist, dissociating themselves from their unassimilated Eastern brethren of the ghetto.

The polyglot population of Vienna, the clash of political and cultural philosophies, the slow dying of the Hapsburg monarchy fed the intellectual currents of the period, at the same time breeding hatreds that burst in Dachau, Bergen-Belsen, and Auschwitz. As *Mein Kampf* shows, the Nazis were to play on the fear and hatred of impoverished Jews whose condition could be blamed on alleged racial degeneracy; but it was the prosperous Jew who was feared the most. Jews like Freud and Schoenberg, who had assimilated partly or fully (and even changed their religion), suffered hatred and injustice as keenly as their less fortunate brethren, and responded with anger and justified resentment. "As a Jew," Freud stated in 1926, "I was prepared to join the Opposition and to do without agreement with the 'compact majority.'" (XX, 274)

IV   *The Founding of Psychoanalysis*

The pivotal event in the development of psychoanalysis was Freud's discovery in 1897 that "psychical reality" exists in its own right and perhaps independently of "actual reality." Freud is popularly thought to have discovered the "unconscious" at this time; but, in fact, the formulation of the unconscious as popularly conceived was a complex process extending over a number of years, beginning with his association with Breuer in the early 1880's.

In November, 1882 Breuer told Freud of a patient, Anna O., whom he had begun treating in 1880, and whose hysterical symptoms he had been able to cure through a combination of hypnosis and a return through word association to the circumstances in which the symptoms had appeared. This "cathartic method" or "talking cure" indicated that a state of mind other than consciousness not only controlled hysterical symptoms but could be reached and influenced, and that ideas connected with words were integral to that state. Freud's experiences in Paris confirmed this discovery, though Charcot stressed the organic causes of hysteria, giving little weight to ideas as symptom-forming. In 1893 Freud joined with Breuer in a "Preliminary Communication" which stressed that symptoms form in "hypnoid" states, are stored in a "second" or "hypnoid" consciousness, can influence conscious behavior (and indeed take it over), and can be alleviated or removed when expressed in words connected to the original traumatic experience. Freud thus was giving greater weight to ideas—that is, to psychological causes—than did Charcot. Freud and Breuer's *Studies on Hysteria* (1895) went beyond the "Preliminary Communication" in identifying the "sexual instinct" as "the most powerful source" of neurosis (II, 200), in stressing the role of repression and stating unequivocally that "unconscious ideas exist and are operative," and that there exists "a splitting of psychical activity" (II, 221).

Freud had used hypnosis for a time in his medical practice, as we noted, wholly discarding it in 1896; he first used the cathartic method in 1889. His technique of unrestricted or "free" association developed between 1892 and 1895. After the publication of *Studies on Hysteria* he proceeded independently of Breuer, their professional collaboration having ended in the summer of 1894. The issue that produced the rupture was Freud's developing view that children have a sexual life independent of any physical trauma or "seduction" they have suffered; in other words, that children generate their own sexual feelings.

Deterred by Charcot's idea that childhood traumas originate in actual experiences and by his own deep-rooted belief that psychical reality is grounded in physiological processes, Freud only gradually came to recognize his error in accepting his patients' statements at face value. "When, however," he states in his autobiography, "I was at last obliged to recognize that these scenes of seduction had never taken place, and that they were only phantasies which my patients had made up or which I myself had perhaps forced on them, I was for some time completely at a loss" (XX, 34). He announced his discovery to Fliess on September 21, 1897; he would not speak it in "the land of the Philistines," but "in your eyes and my own I have more of the feeling of a victory than of a defeat—and, after all, that is not right" (I, 260). He had discovered, in short, that the unconscious is unable to distinguish the true or actual from the fictitious: "impulses" as well as actual events could be repressed.

From this time on, psychical reality was Freud's chief concern; his effort to ground psychology in physiological theory —attempted in a "Project for a Scientific Psychology," begun in 1895 and left unfinished—had virtually ended by the turn of the century. Ideas of this period on repression, the compromise-formations, defense mechanisms, and what Freud later termed the Oedipus complex (first mentioned in a letter to Fliess in October, 1897) were reformulated in later years. Thus, in his 1914 analysis of the "wolf man," he stated the idea of infantile "primal scenes" in light of new insights:

These scenes of observing parental intercourse, of being seduced in childhood, and of being threatened with castration are unquestionably an inherited endowment, a phylogenetic heritage, but they may just as easily be acquired by personal experience. . . . [The child] fills in the gaps in individual truth with prehistoric truth; he replaces occurrences in his own life by occurrences in the life of his ancestors. (XVII, 97)

Drawing on his self-analysis, Freud wrote most of *The Interpretation of Dreams* in the summer of 1899; the book was published at the end of the year in an edition of six hundred copies (the title page is dated 1900). "The book's reception, and the silence since," Freud wrote Fliess, "have once more destroyed any budding relationship with my environment."[12] The book was not ignored, however, and his long isolation was ending; in the years that followed he published some of his most important books including *Psychopathology of Everyday Life* (1901), *Three Essays on Sexuality* and *Jokes and Their Relation to the Unconscious* (1905).

V   *The Psychoanalytic Movement*

From the beginning Freud encountered opposition, which was to grow fierce as the years passed. The theory of infantile sexuality provoked the loudest public clamor. Jones quotes a speaker at a psychiatric congress held in Hamburg in 1910: "This is not a topic for discussion at a scientific meeting, it is a matter for the police."

Following the publication of his books on dreams and parapraxes, Freud's reputation began to grow. In 1902 he invited Alfred Adler, Wilhelm Stekel, Max Kahane, and Rudolf Reitler to meet at his home for discussions. This "Psychological Wednesday Society" expanded, established a library (later destroyed by the Nazis), and in 1908 became the Vienna Psychoanalytical Society. Freud's ideas were being applied by Eugen Bleuler, the head of the psychiatric clinic of the University of Zurich, and by his associate Carl Jung; and a psychoanalytic association formed in Zurich in 1907. Associations formed in other cities in later years, and the American Psychoanalytic Association was formed in 1911. The first international psychoanalytic conference took place in Salzburg in 1908, and in other cities in 1910 and the years immediately preceding World War I. Freud's immediate circle gradually increased, with the addition of Otto Rank in 1906; and Jung, Karl Abraham, Sandor Ferenczi, and Max Eitingon in 1907. His association with Ernest Jones began in 1908.

The first psychoanalytic periodical, the *Jahrbuch für psychoanalytische und psychopathologische Forschungen* (Yearbook for Psychoanalytic and Psychopathological Researchers), was founded in 1908 and was edited by Jung (it ceased publication in 1913); the *Zentralblatt für Psychoanalyse* (Journal for Psychoanalysis), edited at first by Adler and Stekel, first appeared in 1910; *Imago*, specializing in cultural ideas, was established in 1911; the *Zeitschrift für Psychoanalyse* (Journal for Psychoanalysis) in 1912; and the *International Journal of Psychoanalysis* in 1920. The first psychoanalytic publishing house was established in 1919.

The reasons for Freud's rupture with Adler and Stekel in 1911 and 1912 were personal as well as professional. Aware of their feeling of rivalry with their Zurich colleagues, Freud made them joint editors of the *Zentralblatt* and appointed Adler president of the Vienna Society, but Adler's "heresy"—his insistence that neurosis is to be explained by the sense of inferior masculinity, his explanation of sexual striving as a form of "masculine protest," and his virtual dismissal of repression and infantile sexuality —made the rupture with Freud inevitable. Freud disliked Stekel's egotism, though he recognized his occasional brilliance, characterizing him as a pig finding truffles. [13]

There is no doubt that Jung's Swiss background contributed to Freud's regard for him as his intellectual heir and most brilliant colleague. Freud believed that psychoanalysis would have to become an international movement if it was to survive, and Bleuler and Jung had enlarged his circle at a crucial time. Bleuler and Freud first corresponded in 1904; Jung and Freud in 1906. They met for the first time in 1907, and in 1909 Jung travelled with Freud and Ferenczi to the United States, where Freud lectured at, and received an honorary doctorate from, Clark University. Anxious to cement a relationship with his younger colleague, Freud tended to smooth over intellectual differences. Their recently published correspondence, in which Freud more than once takes note of his tendency to be authoritarian, clearly reveals this desire. [14]

Their differences finally surfaced toward the end of 1911 when Freud took critical note that Jung was proposing a libido that was "identical with any kind of desire" (November 30, 1911). Like Adler, Jung had increasingly minimized the role of sexuality in neurosis, to the extent that he was avoiding discussion with his patients of their sexual life. In 1909 he had written Jones, "in publicly announcing certain things one would saw off the branch on which civilization rests; one undermines the impulse to sublimation."[15] On December 18, 1912, following a gradual cooling of their friendship, he wrote Freud an insulting letter that invited a rupture:

You go around sniffing out all the symptomatic actions in your vicinity, thus reducing everyone to the level of sons and daughters who blushingly admit the existence of their faults. Meanwhile you remain on top as the father, sitting pretty. For sheer obsequiousness nobody dares to pluck the prophet by the beard and inquire for once what you would say to a patient with a tendency to analyze the analyst instead of himself.

Their correspondence ended soon afterwards, Freud deeply hurt. Jung ceased editing the *Jahrbuch* and in 1914 resigned from the International Association.

The considerable dissension in the opening years of the movement resulted in part from Freud's strong intellectual pride as founder of a great scientific theory and in part from the desire of strong-minded "sons" who wished to pursue their independent ways. To avoid further schism and to provide a means for orderly revision of ideas, a committee was formed in 1912, consisting of Jones, Rank, Ferenczi, Hanns Sachs, Abraham, and, later, Max Eitingon.

VI   *The Last Years*

Though Freud would not have defined his outlook as pessimistic, the war years, his increasing illness, and his daughter Sophie's death from influenza in 1920, intensified his sense of the tragic. In 1925 he wrote Lou Andreas-Salomé:

The "detachment of old age," I think it is called. It must be connected with a decisive turn in the relationship of the two instincts postulated by me. . . . The never-ceasing pressure of a vast number of unpleasant sensations must have accelerated this otherwise perhaps premature condition, this tendency to experience everything *sub specie aeternitatis*.[16]

His personal suffering had been great during the war. He had worried intensely about his sons serving in the army (Martin was eventually taken prisoner); food was in short supply; the rooms of his apartment and the adjoining office were unheated during two severe winters. In the post-war inflation, he lost his life savings, and it was not until the end of 1920 that he was again earning a moderate income and depositing fees in foreign money in a bank abroad.

A momentous effect of the war was his experience with traumatized war veterans, whom he observed in the Vienna General Hospital, at the invitation of a military commission investigating alleged mistreatment of patients. His observation led to the formulation of the "death instinct," stated in the epochal *Beyond the Pleasure Principle* (1920). *Group Psychology and the Analysis of the Ego* (1921), *The Ego and the Id* (1923), *Inhibitions, Symptoms and Anxiety* (1926), and *Civilization and Its Discontents* (1929) introduced new speculations of an increasingly philosophical cast.

The death of Sophie's young son Heinz, of tuberculosis in 1923, was another deeply felt loss. Freud himself was now seriously ill. In the same year he was operated on for a leucoplakia of the jaw and palate, which proved to be cancerous. The entire upper jaw and palate on the diseased side of the mouth had to be removed. As a result Freud's speech and hearing became impaired, and eating was so painful that he preferred to take his meals alone. Adding to his suffering was an angina attack in 1926. Precancerous tissue was excised in a series of operations; in 1936 cancer was again definitely found.

Freud continued to see patients and to write during these years, though his activities were curtailed. He attended his last international conference in 1923. His break with Rank and the cooling of his friendship with Ferenczi after 1929 brought a new sense of isolation. In 1930 his mother died at the age of ninety-five. He wrote Arnold Zweig in December of that year: "We are moving towards dark times: the apathy of old age ought to enable me to rise above it all, but I cannot help the fact that I am sorry for my seven grandchildren."[17]

The Nazi horrors were soon upon him. His books were publicly burned in Germany in 1933; in 1936 stocks in the publishing house in Leipzig were seized. Though Freud might have left Austria for the safety of another country, he did not. A week later the *Anschluss* in March, 1938, members of the S. A. entered his apartment, were confronted by his wife and daughter Anna, and finally by Freud himself; having been shown a safe, they left with a large sum of money. A week later the Gestapo searched the apartment and arrested his daughter, releasing her in the evening. Through the intervention of President Roosevelt and perhaps Mussolini, Freud and members of his family and two servants were permitted to leave the country (June 4, 1938). Later efforts to bring out his four sisters were unsuccessful. They were eventually imprisoned and murdered in Theresienstadt and Auschwitz.

Freud and his family passed through France, arriving in England at the end of June. He was publicly honored and signed the Charter Book of the Royal Society to which he had been appointed a Corresponding Member in 1938. He lived and practiced in London to the end of his life. The *New Introductory Lectures* had been published in 1933; *Moses and Monotheism*, begun in 1934, was completed and published in 1939. His final major work, the *Outline of Psychoanalysis*, was left unfinished and published in 1940. A recurrence of cancer in February, 1939, proved inoperable, and Freud died seven months later on September 23.

VII   *Freud's Character and Literary Interests*

We indicated earlier that Freud was highly gifted linguistically. He translated five books in his lifetime, including a volume of Charcot and essays of Mill. He once stated that he wished in youth to become a novelist; he read the English novelists widely, chiefly Fielding (*Tom Jones*), Sterne, Dickens, Thackeray, George Eliot, Disraeli. He was, of course, widely read in German fiction. Though he enjoyed the theater, he was indifferent to music (Mozart's operas were an exception). He collected antiquities, an interest fostered by his many trips abroad, including seven visits to Rome, the first in 1901.

At the University of Vienna he had read philosophy and studied Aristotelian logic with the distinguished Franz Brentano; however his knowledge of philosophy seems not to have been profound, and his reading in it was occasional. In later years he did more reading, seeking correspondences between his own ideas and those of Schopenhauer and others. He was particularly fond of citing similarities with Kant, thus his reference in the preface to *Totem and Taboo* to the "categorical imperative" as a compulsive and unconscious force (XIII, viii).[18] He was even more interested in writers who supported his belief in purposive thinking (a theme of Kant's *Critique of Judgment*), and in 1916 began a reading of Lamarck's *Philosophie Zoologique*, seeking to adapt those ideas to psychoanalysis. The Lamarckian concept of "fitness" could, he thought, be equated with the Schopenhauerian will to power and ultimately with the psychoanalytic omnipotence of thought.[19]

One mental quality in Freud is often stressed by those who knew him well: his single-minded and ardent attachment to people and ideas. The literary interests noted were probably as single-minded as his intellectual habits. Stefan Zweig characterized the latter in these words:

Unless Freud understands a thing promptly and unconditionally, it remains unacceptable to him; and no one can explain anything to him unless, of his own self, he can grasp it without reserve. He is thus unfailingly autocratic and intransigent; and it is above all when he is at war, fighting alone against a multitude, that there develops the unqualified pugnacity of a nature ready to face overwhelming odds.[20]

His personal as well as his intellectual judgments tended to be unqualified at first, for, in the words of Joan Riviere, "whatever he perceived was valid in itself." She adds:

He established an instantaneous, direct relation to his perception, which automatically excluded cut-and-dried assumptions, or *arrière-pensées*. Second thoughts and suspended judgment only came much later. The impulse to reject and dismiss at first sight was singularly lacking in him.[21]

If Freud looked upon himself as a conquistador in the realm of science, he also understood that he needed to hold this attitude:

It has always seemed to me that ruthlessness and arrogant self-confidence constitute the indispensable condition for what, when it succeeds, strikes us as greatness; and I also believe that one ought to differentiate between greatness of achievement and greatness of personality.[22]

In *Group Psychology* he defends his sexual theories with the statement that he dislikes "concessions to faintheartedness," adding that "he who knows how to wait need make no concessions" (XVIII, 91).

His intellectual aggressiveness undoubtedly compensated for what he identified in Woodrow Wilson, and perhaps feared in himself, as a deeply rooted "passivity." Rieff suggests that rationality for Freud is the male or active principle under the restriction of the (feminine) emotions: "Freedom is not emotional but rational, not a passion but a strategy, not feminine but masculine, not static but evolutionary."[23] Jones indicates that Freud suffered from hypochondria, intestinal trouble, migraine, sinusitis, and the fear of early death—signs perhaps of continuing neurosis. His hypersensitivity to racial slurs—evident in his statement to Karl Abraham that Jews need a certain amount of masochism to get along in the world—surely intensified these qualities.[24]

All of these contributed to Freud's rationalism, best defined as a heightened and sustained awareness of possible courses of action, without commitment to a final course. Underlying this rationalism is the Kantian assumption that the mind is fitted to know the world—expressed by Freud in his statement (in *Future of an Illusion*) that the mind "has been developed precisely in the attempt to explore the external world" (XXI, 55). "The Project" of 1895 was an aborted effort to find out how this was so. Despite his many statements of faith in reason, he hesitated to promote a thoroughgoing rationalism, in part because he had shown the "reality principle" to be a defense of the "pleasure principle" against the inexorable demands of the world. The forces that man struggles against in the external world are impersonal, not asking man to pledge his allegiance. He stood less in wonder than did Kant at "the starry heavens above me and the moral law within me." "I know that every one of us represents a fragment of life energy," he wrote the American psychologist James J. Putnam in 1915, "but I don't see what energy has to do with freedom, i.e. absence of conditioning factors."[25]

VIII   *The Autobiographical Writings*

Freud's biographer has a wide range of primary materials to draw upon—not only the letters but also numerous personal comments in those works that drew on Freud's self-analysis.[26] The autobiographical writings considered together are remarkable for their paucity of detail and personal reticence. These characteristics are justified in the autobiographical study of 1925, written for a medical history consisting of accounts by leading physicians. They are surprising in the 1914 history, given Freud's express purpose to counter a "cool act of usurpation" of those who were insisting that Breuer was the co-founder of psychoanalysis:

I have never heard that Breuer's great share in psychoanalysis has earned him a proportionate measure of criticism and abuse. As I have long recognized that to stir up contradiction and arouse bitterness is the inevitable fate of psychoanalysis, I have come to the conclusion that I must be the true originator of all that is particularly characteristic in it. (XIV, 8)

Perhaps this reticence is best explained by Freud's belief that psychoanalysis fulfilled its destiny because he was prepared to work in isolation and darkness as its single discoverer. Lesser men like Breuer and Jung, frightened by what they saw in the "underworld" revealed by psychoanalysis, hastened to scramble out (XIV, 22, 66). His major theme is that the process of discovery was a heroic endeavor. When he looked back to "those lonely years, away from the pressures and confusions of today, it seems like a glorious heroic age" (XIV, 22). And that was because his frustration forced him to hold back and, as Charcot advised, "to look at the same things again and again until they themselves begin to speak" (XIV, 22). Adler and Jung lacked this power to look into the depths and accept what they found. Jung had been able to overcome his racial prejudices and, like Adler, do original thinking; but both succumbed to the repression that often befell those who could not overcome their resistance to truth. With their secession, Freud felt it necessary to give up self-restraint and come to intellectual blows with those who threatened his work: "I have no choice in the matter . . . only indolence or cowardice could lead one to keep silence, and silence would cause more harm than a frank revelation of the harms that already exist" (XIV, 49). His theories would attain the massive coherence of an edifice, slowly emerging from clouds of ignorance, and Freud thinks worth quoting the remark of an opponent that the structure of psychoanalysis was similar to that of the Catholic Church in its "internal solidity" (XIV, 27).

By contrast, the autobiography is neither polemical nor defensive. Freud was aware that he had revealed little about himself; for in the postscript of 1935 he indicates that the public had "no claim to learn any more of my personal affairs—of my struggles, my disappointments, and my successes," even though he had been far more candid in some of his works than most of his contemporaries. "I have had small thanks for it, and from my experience I cannot recommend anyone to follow my example" (XX, 73). He was referring surely to *Interpretation of Dreams* in which he presented the most personal thoughts and dream material with total candor and, as in *Psychopathology of Everyday Life*, considerable humor. As in this statement in the autobiography, Freud is occasionally mordant and ironic.

Consistent with the approach he took in the history, Freud is chiefly concerned with showing that the source of scientific greatness lies in the power to generalize results and not merely record phenomena; thus dream analysis advanced psychoanalysis to "the starting-point of a new and deeper science of the mind" which would be indispensable in the study of normal behavior. Its path "led far afield, into spheres of universal interest" (XX, 47). All personal considerations are stripped away in the autobiography to keep this idea before the reader.

Since Freud has been widely criticized for his immodesty and self-publicizing, we can do no better than conclude with a pertinent statement of Paul Roazen:

Freud was entitled as a theorist to decide which aspects of his work were essential to further exploration. The existence of a system of thought which was capable of having "corner-stones" made it possible for disciples to assemble around Freud. The capacity to have disciples says much about the systematic character of a man's mind. To demand of a thinker that he be boldly original as well as intellectually passive is asking to have one's cake and eat it too.[27]

But Freud himself must be given the last word:

But I think I can say in my defense that an intolerant man, dominated by an arrogant belief in his own infallibility, would never have been able to maintain his hold upon so large a number of intellectually eminent people, especially if he had at his command as few practical attractions as I had. (XX, 53)

CHAPTER 2

A Short Account of Freud's Ideas

I Nineteenth-Century Psychology and Scientific Thought

A LEGACY of the European Enlightenment was the debate in the nineteenth century over the nature of mind. The mechanical or mechanistic view—that the human organism is merely a complex machine and that soul or mind are special motions of matter—had exerted great influence on eighteenth-century thought. The opposing view—the vitalistic one—is that the human organism is animated by a force or soul that cannot be explained through the motions of matter.

There were a number of vitalistic philosophies in the nineteenth century. One of them was the pantheistic *Naturphilosophie*, developed by the German philosopher Schelling, that identified a universal "nature" with a universal "mind" or "world ego," and reason with the efflorescence of unconscious, seething forces. These ideas tended to discourage the experimental method and to foster purposive rather than merely descriptive explanation in the sciences. Goethe, for example, spoke of organs performing "the precept of Nature"—Nature containing ideal patterns on which living bodies model themselves.[1] This kind of purposive explanation is typical also of Lamarckian evolution and differs from the Darwinian which states that functional organs form accidental modifications that prove to be favorable in the struggle to live.

A rival to *Naturphilosophie* was the "physico-mathematical method" associated with Helmholtz, Brücke, and others. Freud's teacher Brücke, whose *Lectures on Physiology* (1874) he had studied, distinguished organisms from machines on the basis of their capacity to assimilate energy: a mechanical force—physical energy—alone accounts for the evolution of forms. The general nineteenth-century view of the unconscious is that it is the reservoir of unknown desires, according to Schopenhauer, blind Will itself. There were, however, physiological theories. Johann Herbart (1776–1841) distinguished between levels of consciousness or thresholds; ideas removed from consciousness could influence behavior from below the "dynamic" threshold. G. T. Fechner (1801–87) developed these ideas in his *Elements of Psychophysics* (1860), stating that "What is below the threshold *carries* the consciousness," and comparing the mind to an iceberg. Freud's teacher, and later opponent, Theodor Meynert, developed his own theory of the primary, unconscious "ego" and the secondary, conscious "ego" which "inhibits" or controls the first.

When Freud worked in the psychiatric wards of the Vienna General Hospital, psychiatric ideas depended mainly on physiological theory: mental disturbances were diseases of the normally functioning mind, deriving from fatigued processes or neurotic "constitution." Charcot held similar views. Even after he came to the primacy of psychological causes of hysteria, Freud continued to distinguish between "actual" neuroses originating in physiological disturbances and the psychoneuroses, or simply the neuroses, which accounted for most hysterias and obsessional states. Though he affirmed the importance of physiological explanations throughout his life, and in the "Project" of 1895 sought to ground psychology in neurological theory, Freud depended on assumptions resembling the vitalistic theory. For in distinguishing a psychological reality, he assumed a power of mind independent of and directing physical states.

II   *Freud's Changing Views on the Unconscious*

Though Freud is usually identified with the Unconscious and the Conscious, this distinction is less important than that between the primary and secondary processes, elaborated in *The Interpretation of Dreams*. The primary process resembles the earlier nineteenth-century reservoir of the passions; it is without time or sense of cause and effect and seeks merely to discharge excitations. The secondary process develops when this discharge is frustrated; it seeks to bind these energies as a way of dealing with the sources of frustration. The processes associated with dreaming—condensation and duplication of ideas and images, the reversal of time and space relationships—are characteristic of primary thinking. Secondary thinking is the "common sense," logical thinking of our everyday experience.

The primary process constitutes the Freudian "unconscious," whereas the secondary process, according to the 1913 essay "The Unconscious," is both preconscious and conscious. Preconscious means that portions of our mental experience are not immediately present to consciousness but can be recalled easily; an unconscious thought is difficult to make conscious because it is under repression arising from a conflict in desires, some of which would interfere with our normal functioning in the real world if admitted to consciousness.[2] These repressed wishes can and do enter consciousness when ways are found to remove the repression. Thus when we remember a dream, we actually remember the original wish-fulfilling content only after it has been transformed—its forbidden content sufficiently disguised—so that it can enter consciousness.

The "governing principle" of primary and secondary thinking is the "pleasure [*Lust*] principle." In his 1911 essay formulating this idea, Freud states that the original unlimited gratification of infancy had to give way to the "reality ego" as a way of conserving the means of pleasure—of making it possible in other ways:

> With the introduction of the reality principle one species of thought-activity was split off; it was kept free from reality-testing and remained subordinated to the pleasure principle alone. This activity is *phantasying*, which begins already in children's play, and later, continued as *day-dreaming*, abandons dependence on real objects. (XII, 222)

Freud's dissatisfaction with features of this theory led him to the structural hypothesis, fully stated in 1923. The primary process is now termed the "id." The "ego," comprising those functions like perception and memory that deal with the real world, is originally a "pleasure ego" and part of the id that takes shape as it becomes organized; at its most differentiated, it is identical with the secondary process. Various earlier ideas come together:

. . . the ego seeks to bring the influence of the external world to bear upon the id and its tendencies, and endeavors to substitute the reality principle for the pleasure principle which reigns unrestrictedly in the id. For the ego, perception plays the part which in the id falls to instinct. The ego represents what may be called reason and common sense, in contrast to the id, which contains the passions. (XIX, 25)

The conception of the "reality principle" as the instrument of the "pleasure principle" has undergone a change, for psychoanalysis is defined as "an instrument to enable the ego to achieve a progressive conquest of the id" (XIX, 56).

Whereas the ego is developed fully by the age of three, the superego begins to develop at five or six and becomes fully functioning about the time of puberty. The superego is what we ordinarily mean by conscience; it consists of precipitates of our experience—the images and voices of parents and their substitutes that we have loved and must surrender, images internalized as a way of gratifying the id which will tolerate no loss. The superego is therefore anchored in the id:

Thus in the id, which is capable of being inherited, are harbored residues of the existences of countless egos; and, when the ego forms its superego out of the id, it may perhaps only be reviving shapes of former egos and be bringing them to resurrection. (XIX, 38)

Freud was answering the important question of where "mind" comes from: it is an inherited acquisition, comprising residues of past experiences, each individual recapitulating the history of his ancestors in maturing into an adult.

Identification—the mechanism through which the superego is formed—is only one of the mechanisms by which the ego deals with the demands of the id and threats from the external world. Among other mechanisms are projection (transferring unadmitted desires to another person), isolation (unconsciously segregating one thought from others in the mind), regression (returning to gratifications of earlier stages of development), and repression. The ego also may utilize reaction formation, the process of holding one emotion or attitude in abeyance by stressing another (becoming overly concerned with the happiness of another person as a way of denying hate), or sublimation, the process of transforming a dangerous impulse into a socially useful activity.

III *The Libido*

The definition of "libido" depended on what instincts, or more properly "instinctual drives" [*Triebe*], were thought to be. Instinct in man differs from that in lower animals in which stimulation leads to a direct physical response. Freudian instinct need not do so, which is why Freud believed the concept stood "on the frontier between the mental and the somatic" (XIV, 122). Libido itself was eventually defined as "the force by which the sexual instinct is represented in the mind" (XVII, 137).[3]

Freud tended to distinguish between the libidinal or sexual instinct and the egoistic, self-preservative instinct. In an essay of 1910 he referred directly to "the instincts which subserve sexuality, the attainment of sexual pleasure, and those other instincts, which have as their aim the self-preservation of the individual —the ego-instincts" (XI, 214). This assumption of dual instincts was temporarily upset by his suggestion in his 1914 essay on narcissism that the ego instincts are libidinal through their original attachment to the sexual instincts; in "Instincts and Their Vicissitudes" (1915) he suggested that some of the sexual instincts are permanently associated with the ego instincts. This formulation upset, or at least removed an underpinning of, Freud's view that man was in a state of perpetual conflict with himself. To preserve the dual instinct theory, he would have to demonstrate the existence of non-narcissistic—that is, non-libidinal—parts of the ego. The way was shown in the latter essay in the statement that aggressiveness is a component of the ego and is to be distinguished from the sexual instinct (XIV, 137). Freud thus had anticipated his most controversial theory: his formulation (in 1920) of the notions of the Life Instinct (Eros) and the Death Instinct.

He arrived at his new theory as a result of his discovery of the compulsion to repeat painful experiences; the wounded soldiers he observed in Vienna were re-experiencing war trauma in their dreams. According to his earlier theory, the pleasure principle seeks to lessen and stabilize tension; dreams (punishment dreams as well) achieve this purpose. Traumatic dreams clearly violated this theory. "What wishful impulse could be satisfied by harking back in this way to this exceedingly distressing traumatic experience?" Freud wondered (XXII, 28).

The answer was to be found "beyond the pleasure principle,"

in the death instinct which intermingles and fuses with the erotic or life instinct as the mind develops. Owing to this fusion, neither instinct ordinarily manifests itself in its pure state. The death instinct seeks "to conduct the restlessness of life into the stability of the inorganic state" (XIX, 160); whereas the libido has the job of neutralizing the death instinct by directing it to the musculature, as an aggressive shield, hence the identification of aggression with the death instinct. That part of the instinct that serves the sexual function is "true sadism," and that bound within the organism, "the original erotogenic masochism" (XIX, 163). Indeed this primal sadism is to be identified with masochism.

Freud believed that the suppression of the instincts in the name of civilization inevitably leads to the "revulsion of sadism against the self"; the superego also absorbs the destructiveness of civilization. Freud concluded, in the important essay "The Economic Problem of Masochism" (1924): "The sadism of the superego and the masochism of the ego supplement each other and unite to produce the same effects" (XIX, 170). He found in this phenomenon the explanation for why the greater the restraint a person's aggressiveness is under, the harsher his conscience. His libido theory had thus evolved into a totally pessimistic view of man:

It is consequently left to the individual to decide how he can obtain, for the sacrifice he has made, enough compensation to enable him to preserve his mental balance. On the whole, however, he is obliged to live psychologically beyond his means, while the unsatisfied claims of his instincts make him feel the demands of civilization as a constant pressure upon him. (XIX, 219)

IV Infantile Sexuality and the Oedipus Complex

Sexuality meant for Freud more than the various forms of genital activity. The infantile body is capable of many kinds of pleasure, including sucking, eating, and defecating, and Freud considered these to be erotic in the gratification they provide owing to their connection with the erotogenic zones of the mouth and anus. Accordingly, the period of a child's life up to about a year and a half is termed the oral phase, because the mouth provides the chief pleasure, and the period from one and a half to three, the anal phase, because of the increasing primacy of pleasure derived from excretion. The activities of the oral and anal phases develop psychological functions important in later childhood and adult life: eating, a drawing-in, is the source or prototype of identification; defecation, the retaining and riddance of waste matter, is the prototype of ambivalence.

The genital organs become primary during the third year but do not replace the mouth and anus as sources of pleasure. Though the capability of orgasm emerges at puberty, genital masturbation and phantasies occur in this early phallic stage, ending at about six, at which time a latency period lasting until puberty ensues. None of the early attachments of libido (cathexes) are fully abandoned; indeed, they come to play an important role in mature sexuality as "fore-pleasure." It is possible, however, for regression to earlier infantile attachments to occur, perhaps as a result of the failure to overcome the Oedipus complex. The libido may also remain fixated at these earlier stages. Character is defined in the terms of these developmental stages. Thus a rapacious or stingy person is said to exhibit an "anal-sadistic" temperament. Thrift, neatness, and obstinacy are promoted by anal erotism, ambition by a strongly urethral-erotic character.

In understanding the Oedipus complex, it must be remembered that at least up to the phallic period, the opposition in boys and girls is between active and passive qualities, not between male and female sexual differences. In the phallic period, only the male genital organ is important—present or absent—in both sexes. One of Freud's basic assumptions is that men and women are bisexual and, in the phallic stage, entertain sexual phantasies involving both parents. These phantasies have to do with seduction by, and coition with, the parents. Certain of these phantasies, chiefly those involving coition and castration, are "primal" or inherited.

The course of the Oedipus complex is the following. During the phallic or oedipal phase (between three and six), boys and girls wish to supplant the father in the mother's affection (as Oedipus unknowingly did when he slew his father and married his mother) and also to supplant the mother in the father's affection and bear him a child (if birth is connected with sexual activity). Whether observing the missing penis in girls or drawing on inherited reinforced knowledge, the boy is forced by fear of cas-

tration to give up the Oedipal wish. Alternatively, he faces sacrifice of his penis if he takes the mother's role in coition. The girl
originally mistakes her clitoris for the penis and treats it as such,
but she soon learns the difference, as a result feeling shame and
jealousy or "penis envy." Eventually she identifies with her
mother and adopts the feminine role, accepting a baby as a substitute for the missing organ. Her strong dependence on the
father is based on an equally strong early dependence on the
mother. The bisexuality of women is, in fact, more prominent
owing to their two sexual zones—the vagina and the clitoris.

With the onset of the latency period, genital masturbation ordinarily ends or decreases, as do the associated phantasies,
though remnants live on as daydreams. An important consequence of the dissolution of the Oedipus complex is the formation
of the superego, through the internalization of parental imagos.
The period that follows puberty is termed the genital. Sexuality,
though still a source of pleasure, has become "altruistic" in learning to serve the reproductive function.

V *Theory of Neurosis*

Freud's theory of neurosis is complex, and only its main features can be indicated here. Normality, he stated in a 1906 essay,
"is a result of the repression of certain component instincts and
constituents of the infantile disposition and of the subordination
of the remaining constituents under the primacy of the genital
zones in the service of the reproductive function" (VII, 277).
Neurosis results when these component instincts escape repression and enter consciousness as painful symptoms.

Freud distinguished two forms of psychoneurosis—hysteria and
obsessional neurosis. Hysterical symptoms may erupt as phobias,
which Freud tentatively classes with "anxiety hysteria," or they
may erupt as forms of "conversion hysteria," including motor
paralysis, involuntary contractions, and hallucination (XX, 111).
The symptoms of obsessional neurosis eventuate in reaction formations, for example, compulsive neatness and cleanliness. These
formations are explained by the regression of the libido to the
anal-sadistic stage. In hysteria, the regression is to the "primary
incestuous sexual objects" and not to the earlier sexual organization (XVI, 343). Freud concluded in his 1926 study of anxiety that

in hysteria and obsessional neurosis what is "being fended off are the trends of the Oedipus complex" (XX, 114).

If the ego approves the regression to infantile fixations, the component (infantile) instincts need not manifest themselves as painful symptoms. In the perversions, libidinal satisfaction is achieved precisely through regression to infantile sexuality, centering in a single component instinct, as in coprophilia. Perverse gratification can issue in genital orgasm; however the center of the experience is in the forepleasure.

A number of important conclusions about civilization and its institutions derive from Freud's theory of neurosis. His most famous conclusion, perhaps, is that "all the ties that bind people to mystico-religious or philosophico-religious sects and communities are expressions of crooked cures of all kinds of neuroses" (XVIII, 142). If the neurotic is excluded from the group, he creates his own imaginative world and religion, "his own system of delusions, and thus recapitulates the institutions of humanity in a distorted way which is clear evidence of the dominating part played by the directly sexual impulsions" (XVIII, 142). This assumption that there is a sexual basis in group and institutional relationships is a permanent and vital feature of Freud's social psychology.

Indeed, he distinguished pure psychological types according to their libidinal character. In the 1931 essay "Libidinal Types" he cited three types: the erotic, for whom receiving love and depending on those who can deprive one of it are the chief concerns of life; the obsessional, who fear their conscience and depend on themselves; the narcissistic, whose primary concern is self-preservation. Freud related these types to the demands of the id, the superego, and the ego respectively. Mixed types, like the erotic-narcissistic, occur most often and may be most prone to neurosis. Freud concludes that a wholly mixed type—the erotic-obsessional-narcissistic—would no longer be a type but would be "the absolute norm, the ideal harmony" (XXI, 219).

He provided another definition of the "wholly normal, ideal" type in his essay on narcissism. "A real happy love," he states, "corresponds to the primal condition in which object-libido and ego-libido cannot be distinguished" (XIV, 100). But he was seldom willing to state the aims of psychoanalysis in positive terms. There were, first of all, inherent difficulties to be overcome, among them the "gain from illness" which prevents many patients from surrendering very real gratifications, and civilization itself, which works against the achievement of an ideal existence.

Freud surveyed the problem at the Second Psychoanalytical Conference in 1910: "Neuroses have in fact their biological function as a protective contrivance and they have their social justification: the 'gain from illness' they provide is not always a purely subjective one" (XI, 150). Nevertheless the gain from illness was ultimately of no benefit to the individual or society. Insight and release from illness will promote change to a better civilization than now exists. Could psychoanalysis as a therapeutic science define the values by which men and women should live? It did have its "scale of values," Freud wrote Romain Rolland in 1930, "but its sole aim is the enhanced harmony of the ego" which mediates the claims of the id and of external reality.[4] Theoretically, the minimum aim of psychoanalysis is to remove the amnesia of the second to fifth year (XVII, 183); the maximum aim was impossible to state because a healthy civilization is not foreseeable or easily defined.

CHAPTER 3

The Case Histories

I   Studies on Hysteria

FREUD recognized the novelistic character of his early case
histories, commenting at one point on how unscientific they
seemed and how like "short stories" they were, compared with
his work in neuropathology (II, 160). The preface to the first edition indicates why he felt their scientific usefulness was limited:
only "very incomplete evidence" was being presented on the
principal role of sexuality in hysteria. "It is precisely observations
of a markedly sexual nature that we have been obliged to leave
unpublished" (II, xxix). We noted earlier the theoretical significance of these studies. Their importance as literature derives
from Freud's highly personal narrative of discovery in the four
case histories he contributed. Breuer wrote the first; Anna O.,
whom he treated from the end of 1880 to June, 1882, following
the death of her father, developed a series of hysterical
symptoms, including paralysis and contraction of limbs, dysfunc-
tions of speech and sight, dual consciousness of a "real" and evil
self. As we indicated earlier, Breuer was able to overcome the
amnesia responsible for these symptoms through a "talking cure."

The succeeding four cases—Freud's—seem to have been arranged so that the case of most value to Freud was considered
last: it was that of Elisabeth von R., his first complete analysis of
a hysteria. He is, in fact, tracing the process of his discovery of
the analytic method. To this end, he is careful not to summarize
his discoveries before he has presented the facts; he also
dramatizes important episodes to create suspense. The first of the
patients, Emmy von N., suffered from an anxiety neurosis and

phobias, gastric disturbances, and animal dreams. Freud used the "cathartic method" for the first time in treating these symptoms. The second patient, Lucy R., suffered from a marginal hysteria resembling an anxiety neurosis and involving a dysfunction of the sense of smell. The third, Katharina, suffered from hysterical symptoms associated with "virginal anxiety," arising from the sight of her uncle (actually her father) in bed with her cousin and from sexual advances made to her at fourteen. The fourth and last (excluding shorter cases), Elisabeth von R., suffered from hysterical symptoms whose treatment led Freud to the discovery of repression. This patient resembled Anna O. in at least one important way, for a dysfunction of limb had occurred following the death of her father, whom she had nursed. At the time of his illness, she revealed (only after Freud encouraged a free association of memories) she had become interested in a young man in the neighborhood, and Freud concluded that ideas associated with nursing her father had come into conflict with her desire for the young man. "The outcome of this conflict was that the erotic idea was repressed from association and the affect attaching to that idea was used to intensify or revive a physical pain which was present simultaneously or shortly before" (II, 146–47).

If Breuer was shocked by the implications of the sexual aetiology of hysteria (or at least the conclusions Freud later would draw), Freud was at first incredulous—hesitating to seek explanations beyond the physiological. Thus he stressed spinal neurasthenia in Elisabeth von R., though her symptoms suggested deeper causes. His wording is cautious, and though he does not avoid the reference to erotic experience, he prefers to show its effect rather than discuss it at length. In showing its effect, Freud stresses both his astonishment and growth of perception.

Breuer, by contrast, never dramatizes and makes virtually no reference to his personal feelings. He conveys instead an impression of total objectivity and psychological distance (in fact, the treatment ended abruptly when he became aware of the patient's feelings toward him).[1] Freud not only describes the patient fully but dramatizes the encounter and his own feelings:

This lady [Emmy von N.], when I first saw her, was lying on a sofa with her head resting on a leather cushion. She still looked young and had finely-cut features, full of character. Her face bore a strained and painful expression, her eye-lids were drawn together and her eyes cast down;

there was a heavy frown on her forehead and the naso-labial folds were deep. (II, 48)

The economy of the narrative makes it possible for Freud to combine his factual account with his sense of the experience and of intellectual discovery; his stress is often on his intuitive understanding:

When, three days ago, she had first complained about her fear of asylums, I had interrupted her after her first story, that the patients were tied on to chairs. I now saw that I had gained nothing by this interruption and that I cannot evade listening to her stories in every detail to the very end. After these arrears had been made up, I took this fresh crop of fears from her as well. I appealed to her good sense and told her she really ought to believe me more than the silly girl from whom she had had the gruesome stories about the way in which asylums are run. (II, 61)

He also keeps before the reader his sense of the limitations to be overcome, so that each intellectual discovery has the force of a personal conquest, as in his learning how to talk to women about "shameful" matters (II, 132). The demonstration of that frankness—and the intellectual honesty that accompanied it—is an organizing principle of the studies. The concluding discussion of psychotherapy stresses this point implicitly: the total recollection necessary to recovery involves a total frankness, especially in the "personal sacrifice" of the patient in revealing erotic wishes (II, 301). But already a pessimism is evident in the conclusion that the gain from the end of hysterical illness may be nothing more than an arming against "common unhappiness" (II, 305).

II Fragment of an Analysis of a Case of Hysteria (1905)

In the "Dora" analysis (written mostly in 1901), Freud probably had in mind the deficiencies of the *Studies:* "Whereas before I was accused of giving *no* information about my patients, now I shall be accused of giving information about my patients which ought not to be given" (VII, 7). He defends in the preface the need for "all possible frankness" in naming the sexual organs and discussing sexual experiences with the reader as well as with the patient. Only "a singular and perverse prurience," he adds, could assume that the doctor who engages in such discussion could receive sexual gratification from the reported material (VII, 9).

The fullness of Dora's history is, indeed, its most remarkable feature. Freud was not pioneering new ground but rather illustrating the psychoanalytic method more fully than it had hitherto been shown. Only the materials of his own analysis, as these had been presented in *Dreams* five years earlier, came close to being extensive, but these had not been presented systematically. The Dora analysis, though it was broken off, is systematic, demonstrating in a masterful exposition that mental life is wholly determined and that no stray memory or detail is without significance. The case also demonstrates the crucial role of dream analysis in identifying and removing (or almost removing) hysterical symptoms, as well as the therapeutic use of free association. Preliminary techniques employed earlier had been abandoned, and the patient now decided what to discuss in analysis, "and in that way I start out from whatever surface his unconscious happens to be presenting to his notice at the moment" (VII, 12). Freud also discusses the phenomenon of "transference" and, in anticipation of *Three Essays*, demonstrates that one meaning of neurotic symptoms is the representation of "a phantasy with a sexual content" (VII, 47). He was also able to shed light on the perversions and their relation to psychoneurosis and homosexuality in women.

As in the *Studies*, Freud traces his process of discovery in a dramatic and detailed narrative but now gives increasing attention to the patient's developing insight. The narrative is chiefly devoted to Dora's relations with friends of her parents, K. and his wife, who had become her father's mistress, and with whom Dora had formed a warm relationship. When she was fourteen, K. kissed her, and she had broken away in disgust, Freud surmising that she had felt K.'s erection. Two years later, in the course of a walk with K., she slapped his face in the belief he was making another advance and informed her mother as a way of letting her father know. Neurotic symptoms, suffered intermittently from the age of twelve, recurred, chiefly as a nervous cough and a hysterically induced appendicitis. At eighteen the girl threatened suicide; Freud began to treat her at this time. When he suggested that she had unconsciously been assuming K. would divorce his wife and marry her, Dora stopped treatment.

The dream analysis revealed highly complex motives: jealousy of her father's love for K.'s wife, for whom her feeling was homosexual; ambivalent feelings toward the father, who, she believed, had transmitted his venereal disease to her and had given her to K. as payment for his mistress. Through the agency of a governess who had nurtured a distrust of men, Dora had come to fear that all men were unfaithful and diseased; and believing herself to be incapable of dealing with her erotic feeling for K. sought her father's protection and his substitution as a lover. The nervous cough, symptomatic of a number of repressed feelings, was a means of identifying with her father, who suffered from a lung ailment, as well as with his mistress. The cough at the same time expressed her wish to marry K. Her homosexuality derived from her ambivalent feelings toward her father.

Stated in summary fashion and abstractly, these ideas are obscure and bewildering even to the sophisticated modern reader. Their dramatic representation, occupying more than a hundred pages (interspersed with connecting analysis and commentary), illuminates each of the contributing motives and experiences. Freud reproduces in considerable detail the dialog of analysis by which Dora began to approach self-understanding, though the material of the second important dream analyzed is presented in "the somewhat haphazard order in which it recurs to my mind" (VII, 95).

Realizing that most of his readers would find incredible so complex an analysis, particularly of an adolescent girl, Freud continually returns to details that point up seeming contradictions. This approach differs from that of the *Studies*, which reveal similar contradictions but chiefly illustrate the procedure of "clearing away the pathogenic psychical material layer by layer" (II, 139). Nothing in Dora's situation seems logical: her bouts of good health alternating with bouts of illness seem inexplicable. In this way Freud leads the reader to the one necessary explanation: an unconscious sexual aetiology of the neurosis. Though he warns that the analysis is fragmentary, his purpose is realized through the materials available to him. The theme that organizes the case history is the sexual origin of much behavior in life that seems altogether mysterious and inexplicable.

III   *"Little Hans"* (1909)

Five-year-old Hans suffered from a phobia, specifically a fear that a horse would bite him. Analysis at first suggested guilt over masturbation, but the causation proved more complex. On a walk with his mother, Hans had observed an omnibus horse fall to the ground and kick its feet; he thought the horse was dead and assumed from the experience that all horses would fall in this way. At the same time, he identified the fallen horse with his father through a wish to have him die. This experience was associated in his mind with another: he had overheard a warning given to a child that a white horse would bite if a finger was put near its mouth. He also associated loaded carts with feces-laden bodies and loaded furniture vans with pregnant women. The fallen horse thus represented his mother giving birth, as well as his father. The phobia suggested, then, that the hostility toward the father was a screen for his sexual longing for the mother. Earlier jealous feelings that had been suppressed had predisposed the boy to neurotic illness.

The case provided important evidence that emotions occur as "pairs of contraries" and "do not as a rule become simultaneously conscious except at the climaxes of passionate love" (X, 113). If Hans struck his father, he immediately kissed the place struck. The case also provided evidence that anxiety-hysteria is the typical childhood neurosis, that masturbation is important in infancy, that the castration and Oedipus complexes are sources of ambivalence.

Since the theory of infantile sexuality would be greatly strengthened by direct evidence from child analyses, and virtually none were available, Freud considered the case of immense importance and drew upon it in other writings. He was presented, however, with a new and perplexing problem; for he was working with second-hand evidence. Hans had been analyzed by his physician father; Freud had been consulted during the analysis, but he had personally interviewed the boy only once. Anticipating the criticism that these circumstances and the suggestibility of a five-year-old reduced the objectivity and usefulness of the findings, Freud states that these were confirmed by analysis of older patients. He admits that Hans was presented with ideas he could not have expressed himself, but this was not unusual; for patients are frequently presented with "conscious anticipatory ideas" as an aid to recovering unconscious materials. Analysis is a therapeutic process, not "an impartial scientific investigation" (X, 104). Nevertheless, Freud does not hesitate to accept as "unassailable" that Hans knew unconsciously the main facts of conception and childbirth, and he bases this assertion on his play with a doll, a phantasy concerning a younger sister, and his admission that the act of defecating was like having a baby. It is the phantasy that is taken as the "most cogent evidence" (X, 129). But Freud is aware that the sense of cogency depends on experiencing the evidence as it is received: "a final sense of conviction" derives from actual experience and not from reading about it (X, 103).

Such statements reveal a defensiveness about the evidence adduced for so complex a childhood neurosis. At one point Freud argues that even the model child—raised in an enlightened home and seldom disciplined or threatened—could develop a phobia as a way of dealing with unavoidable conflict. Hans, he insists, was not as exceptional a child as his intellectual and sexual precocity might suggest. And Freud turns the argument on his critics:

Where do my opponents obtain their knowledge, which they produce with so much confidence, on the question whether the repressed sexual instincts play a part . . . in the aetiology of the neuroses, if they shut their patients' mouths as soon as they begin to talk about their complexes or their derivatives? For the only alternative source of knowledge remaining open to them are my own writings and those of my adherents. (X, 144)

Though lacking the sense of personal discovery and emotional coloration that distinguishes the earlier histories, the narrative is exceedingly detailed and is presented as ongoing; for Freud wishes to show that infantile sexuality is unmistakably present in the terrifying reality of *reported* phantasies. In other words, reported evidence—whether in the notes of a physician father or in works of literature—has weight if confirmed by *shared* emotional responses of physician and patient, writer and reader. The literary qualities of the case history are an important means for securing this shared response. Another is the establishing of corresponding experiences, as in the 1908 essay on hysterical phantasies. Unconscious phantasies uncovered in analysis correspond not only to "the situations in which satisfaction is consciously obtained by perverts," Freud indicates, but also to the reported behavior of certain famous Roman emperors (IX, 162).

IV "The Rat Man" (1909)

Notes upon a Case of an Obsessional Neurosis complements
"Little Hans" because it distinguishes obsessional from anxiety
neurosis. In it Freud revised his 1896 formulation of obsessional
ideas as the re-emergence of repressed self-reproaches over
childhood sexual acts (X, 221). His new formulation depended on
his growing realization that every neurosis reactivates an infantile
neurosis that had not been serious enough to be recognized—as
he expressed the idea in the "Wolf Man" (XVII, 99). Whereas in
hysteria both the precipitating and the infantile experiences or
"preconditions" are forgotten, in obsessional neurosis the latter
are forgotten sometimes but the precipitating experiences are always remembered—except that the affect is dissociated from the
idea. The neurotic can thus speak of the idea but without feeling
or understanding of its meaning (X, 195–96). Indeed, the loss of
connection between ideas commonly occurs.

Freud also distinguished a second way of defending against the
remembered idea: the employment of "deliria," in which rational
ideas join with irrational ones in a complex way:

They are not purely reasonable considerations arising in opposition to the
obsessional thoughts, but, as it were, hybrids between the two species of
thinking; they accept certain of the premises they are combating, and
thus, while using the weapons of reason, are established upon a basis of
pathological thought. (X, 222)

These defenses make the obsessional neurotic prone to superstition and the acceptance of thoughts as omnipotent; he is also
likely to be ridden with uncertainty and doubt, and to be occupied with death as a means of resolving problems, particularly
those concerning love. These states of mind all exhibit the confusion of mind or dissociation of thought of obsessional neurosis.[2]

The case of the Rat Man confirmed infantile sexuality and shed
further light on the essential role of infantile masturbation in
neurosis. Obsessional acts, Freud was able to show, approximate
masturbatory acts in infancy.

The obsessional neurosis of the thirty-year-old patient originated in "premature sexual activity" occurring between the ages
of four and seven. A succession of experiences with governesses

led to the wish to see women naked and to an accompanying, and conflicting, death wish against his father, with whom he shared an affectionate relationship. A later death wish against his father related to an inheritance that would have made possible his marriage to a poor girl. After the father's death, a conflict between a wish to marry the girl and a wish to satisfy his parents' ideas regarding his marriage precipitated his illness. A frustrating experience in adult life thus had reactivated infantile feelings. Furthermore, the behavior of the patient exhibited various confusions and dissociations of mind connected with obsessional neurosis. While serving in the army, the patient had heard about a sadistic torture employing rats and immediately felt compelled to perform a series of acts—"sanctions" that would have to be fulfilled if both the girl he loved and his father (imagined as living) were to be saved from the torture. Freud was able to show that the rat idea covered a series of notions involving money, the penis, and anal erotism, and the fear of syphilis. The patient had identified with the rat, as a result of his own rat-like behavior as a child and his death wish against the father.

The "Rat Man" is superior to "Dora" and "Little Hans" because Freud was able to carry the analysis to completion and to conduct it himself (his invaluable notes during analysis were published in 1955). Though the analysis is reported as it occurred, Freud dramatizes the facts less than in "Dora," one reason perhaps being that he encountered less resistance, so that interest attached to the details of the neurosis rather than to his encounters with the patient. As a result, there is greater attention to problems of language; Freud shows that the language of obsessional neurosis is related in important ways to the language of conscious thought and demonstrates the continuum of abnormal and normal states and the difficulty of defining these. A particularly important idea is that thinking becomes sexualized in obsessional neurosis, an idea of increasing importance to Freud, as *Totem and Taboo* shows. Because language is a manifestation of unconscious instinctual processes, the associations evident in words make it possible to define the "mind" of a culture and civilization, as well as to dramatize the individual consciousness. The psychoanalytic study of literary works was to follow the lead provided in this case history.

V   *"The Schreber Case" (1911)*

"Psychoanalytic Notes on an Autobiographical Account of a Case of Paranoia," or the "Schreber Case" as this important study is popularly known, was not based on Freud's analysis of the patient; nor was he acquainted with him. He was instead commenting on the 1903 memoirs of a notorious judicial official, Daniel Schreber, who had been under treatment for mental illness in asylums in 1884–85 and in 1893–1902, finally gaining his discharge through legal suit. Written shortly before Schreber's release, the memoirs were of special interest to Freud because they constituted "an ingenious delusional structure" which illustrated the complex mechanisms of paranoia. The literary interest of the case history lies in the rich elaboration of the ideas and their implications for analysis of art and culture.

Schreber's delusion passed through a number of stages. He first phantasized that he was to be turned into a woman through emasculation and used sexually. At first his persecutor was his former doctor, Flechsig; later Schreber phantasized that God was either the initiator or Flechsig's accomplice. For God was pure "nerve," capable of transformation into anything imaginable and consisting of higher and lower realms, each constituting separate Beings. A defect in his Being made Him on rare occasions subject to the influence of men and incapable of seeing them as they were—hence His persecution of Schreber. Schreber finally believed that his emasculation was necessary to the redemption of the world: he now had a mission to repopulate and transform the world as the wife of God. At the climax of his illness he believed the end of the world had come about and that he was the only man alive.

Freud concluded that Schreber's illness was inaugurated by unadmitted homosexual feeling toward Flechsig, whom Schreber identified with an older brother; God was representative of the father. Schreber's way of dealing with his homosexuality was to invest God with voluptuous feelings and to regard emasculation as a means to bring about the rebirth of humanity. Thus Freud found in Schreber confirmation of his theory that unmastered homosexuality is an essential component of paranoia. In contrast to the hysteric whose liberated libido turns into physical disability or anxiety, the paranoiac becomes megalomaniac and continues to perceive the world, at the same time constructing theories to explain changes in it. He has a strong need to recover his relationship to people whom he once loved, even if that relationship is now based on hate. Paradoxically, the delusion is thus "an attempt at recovery, a process of reconstruction" (XII, 71).

The Schreber case, like that of "The Rat Man," reveals Freud's growing interest in the delusional basis of many customs and beliefs. The memoirs presented for analysis a full-blown religious vision which had been widely publicized. Freud was to return to this theme in the later study of Woodrow Wilson.[3] In a postscript (1912), he noted the usefulness of the case in the study of mythology, in particular the use of the sun as a sublimated "father symbol," and indicated his agreement with Jung that "the mythopoeic forces of mankind are not extinct" and "give rise in the neuroses to the same psychical products as in the remotest past ages" (XII, 82).

VI *"The Wolf Man" (1918)*

The analysis that provided the material for one of Freud's most remarkable writings (*From the History of an Infantile Neurosis*) began in 1910 and concluded in 1914. The patient was a Russian man of twenty-three, who had suffered anxiety-hysteria and obsessional neurosis in childhood and a recurrent illness when he was seventeen, and was virtually incapable of taking care of himself when he came to Freud for help. He was treated by Freud again after the war, and twice in later years by another analyst.[4]

Freud undoubtedly considered this case history (written in 1914) his most important since it provided decisive evidence of infantile sexuality—dissension over which had led to his break with Adler and Jung. His reference at the beginning of the history to their "twisted reinterpretations" suggests the strength of his feelings at this time, and in later critical references to them he is indeed defensive about the priority of his discoveries, particularly the inheritance of primal phantasies.

The role of primal phantasy in the illness of the "Wolf Man" is a central consideration; indeed the history contains Freud's most thorough examination of the phenomenon. In the *Introductory Lectures* of 1916–17 he attempted a definitive statement, concluding that primal phantasies are a "phylogenetic endowment":

In them the individual reaches beyond his own experience into primaeval experience at points where his own experience has been too rudimentary. It seems to me quite possible that all the things that are told to us today in analysis as phantasy—the seduction of children, the inflaming of sexual excitement by observing parental intercourse, the threat of castration (or rather castration itself)—were once real occurrences in the primaeval times of the human family, and that children in their phantasies are simply filling in the gaps in individual truth with prehistoric truth. (XVI, 371)

His momentous announcement to Fliess that childhood seductions might have been phantasized could now be extended to the possibility that "the psychology of the neuroses has stored up in it more of the antiquities of human development than any other source" (XVI, 371). But latent in this idea is the pessimism of the next two decades.

The scene of the primal phantasy of the "Wolf Man" was the bedroom of the parents, in which the sleeping year-and-a-half-old child awoke to observe an intercourse performed from behind. So astonishing are the results of this scene that Freud warns the reader at the beginning of the "extraordinary and incredible" nature of the account (XVII, 12). After he builds to a description of the "primal scene" he returns to it frequently to explain other formative experiences. Thus, a year afterwards the impressionable boy saw a servant girl scrubbing the floor on her knees—a position that presumably reminded him of his mother's position in the intercourse. Shortly after he turned three, his sister engaged him in sexual play and told him that his nurse did the same with people like the gardener; as a result he attempted to seduce his nurse by playing with his penis before her. Taking her discouragement of the act as a threat of castration, he reverted to the anal-sadistic stage and gratified himself through cruelty to animals. At the same time his earlier sexual play led him to adopt a passive attitude toward his father, whom he now took as a sexual object and sought to provoke into beatings that would alleviate his guilt.

The result was an anxiety-hysteria suffered at four—evidenced by a dream of six or seven white, immobile staring wolves in a tree outside his bedroom window. Freud interpreted the immobility as a transposition and reversal of the violent motion of the primal intercourse witnessed earlier and concluded that the anxiety produced by the dream (aided by "narcissistic genital libido") led the boy to repudiate his desire for sexual union with the father (XVII, 46). Obsessional symptoms appeared at four-and-a-half, with the introduction of religious ideas; these produced compromise formations connected with anal-erotism and also ambivalent feelings toward his father, whom he now saw as a harsh God. Freud comments that, aside from its pathological effects,

religion achieved all the aims for the sake of which it is included in the education of the individual. It put a restraint on his sexual impulsions by affording them a sublimation and a safe mooring; it lowered the importance of his family relationships, and thus protected him from the threat of isolation by giving him access to the great community of mankind. The untamed and fear-ridden child became social, well-behaved, and amenable to education. (XVII, 114–15)

Analysis of the primal scene led Freud to an understanding of organic disorders connected with feminine impulses and ambivalent feelings toward the mother, the transformations of homosexual feeling, and in general the mechanisms and effects of anal-erotism. Though the end of the obsessional neurosis came at age ten, remnants of it were evident in the diminution of intellectual interests and sublimations (an important consequence of religious ideas). Analysis partially restored these.

The interplay of these many forces is dealt with in Freud's most elaborate and powerful analysis. Consideration of infantile sexuality is subordinated now to that of the primal scene, and is more profound and searching because Freud was able to deal with the primal scene as an external imperative or force that corresponded to the individual phantasies of children.

His phrasing of ideas seeks to establish the correspondence as a necessary one: the primal scene points to an "instinctive endowment" comparable to "the far-reaching *instinctive* knowledge of animals":

This instinctive factor would then be the nucleus of the unconscious, a primitive kind of mental activity, which would later be dethroned and overlaid by human reason, when that faculty came to be acquired, but which in some people, perhaps in everyone, would retain the power of drawing down to it the higher mental processes. Repression would be the return to this instinctive stage, and man would thus be paying for his great new acquisition with his liability to neurosis. . . . (XVII, 120)

The individual is seen here as the pawn of instinctual forces, in perpetual confrontation; once a primal repression occurs, succeeding repressions mount and are undone. The earlier case histories imply this view, but Freud was not to articulate it until his thinking on the instincts and neurosis began to change.

A recent commentator states that Freud's physiological thinking committed him to an "austerely mechanical model" and produced a "rigidly objective style and the emphatically scientistic vocabulary."[5] The histories do not support this characterization entirely or the explanation offered; nor do most of Freud's writings after 1900. The histories at least are written in a highly personal style which, in the manner of Claude Bernard and Descartes, seeks to personalize the act of discovery, and this style was extended to many kinds of exposition throughout Freud's career. Nevertheless, highly technical passages in the objective style noted do occur—arising, however, not from a mechanical view of the mind, but usually from an effort to define the unconscious more exactly. Indeed, the main trend of Freud's thinking—and prose style—was toward the loosening of definition as a means of generalizing his discoveries, applying them to a wide range of cultural problems, and increasing their philosophical import.

The following passage from "The Wolf Man" illustrates Freud's technical style at its least attractive:

The state of affairs . . . after the dream, may be described as follows. The sexual trends had been split up; in the unconscious the stage of the genital organization had been reached, and a very intense homosexuality set up; on the top of this (virtually in the conscious) there persisted the earlier sadistic and predominantly masochistic sexual current; the ego had on the whole changed its attitude towards sexuality, for it now repudiated sexuality and rejected the dominant masochistic aims with anxiety, just as it had reacted to the deeper homosexual aims with the formation of a phobia. (XVII, 111–12)

Subtle changes have occurred in style since *Dreams* and other works of that period. The statement is simultaneously categorizing and picturesque, as in earlier writings; but abstraction and image are fused and not merely joined as loose metaphor. Though Freud recognized that topographical distinctions belie the nature of mind, figurative language permitted him to stress what was common in psychological experience rather than what was different. In other words, Freud's style was increasingly shaped by rhetorical and not merely intellectual considerations or assumptions about the nature of mind.

But one intellectual consideration should be stressed: no statement can be or should be taken as final. Ricoeur has shown in a definitive analysis how Freud's misapprehension about childhood seductions shaped the language of *Dreams*: if these seductions were actual memories, the regression to them in dreams was formal and therefore spatial; if, however, the seductions were more often phantasized, the representation of mind would be greatly altered.[6] Freud's shock at his mistake helps to explain why he is concerned with affirming the existence of certain mental phenomena like repression without claiming to have established a single authentic scientific discourse. In allowing contradictions to show, he was building a truly dialectical structure of ideas from which general correspondences and unifying concepts would emerge.

Perhaps the most fruitful approach to Freud's characteristic thinking and prose is through Emile Benveniste's characterization of the language of analysis itself:

The analyst operates with what the subject tells him, he views the subject in the discourses that the latter makes, he examines him in his locutory and "story-making" behavior, and through these discourses there is slowly shaped for him another discourse that he must make explicit, that of the complex buried within the unconscious. The analyst, therefore, will take the discourse as a stand-in for another "language" which has its own rules, symbols, and syntax and which refers back to underlying structures of the psychism.[7]

This attitude of the analyst toward language is Freud's in his writing: he addresses the reader as patient in his role as analyst, and in doing so gives to each subject its appropriate language that must be true to the moment of discovery in its full complexity. This means that Freud wishes to tell us how as scientist and analyst he arrived at his discovery, to show how a translation is made at the moment of discovery from one kind of discourse into another, and to prepare us for a new way of thinking about ourselves. Staking the essay to the moment of discovery is a way of keeping track of origins and of preventing insight from disappearing into impersonal and reductive formulation.

CHAPTER 4

The Interpretation of Dreams *and Other Theoretical Writings*

I   The Interpretation of Dreams

NO masterpiece of scientific thought reveals more of its author or is written in a more personal style than *The Interpretation of Dreams*. Freud planned and wrote it in the late 1890's; and though he added and deleted a considerable amount of material through eight editions, the structure of the argument remained the same, and the personal note persisted; for critical remarks on Adler, Stekel, and Jung abound in the later editions. Though the work contains what Freud regarded as some of his most enduring discoveries, it is also a revelation of personal conflict and neurosis—more consciously planned, perhaps, than many commentators have assumed. His "splendid isolation" from his scientific colleagues and the intense relationship with Fliess freed him for a creative effort that, for the first time, joined thought and feeling by allowing ideas to unfold as they were discovered and felt.

Freud's dream theory is best understood in its mature form, and we shall consider it as such. Dreams are a form of wish fulfillment originating in the unconscious (or id) as a wish that momentarily escapes repression, or in what remains unfinished in preconscious waking activity. One purpose of dreams is to maintain sleep—a need of the conscious ego that Freud, in the *Outline*, identifies with "an instinct to return to the intra-uterine life that has been abandoned" (XXIII, 166; IV, 234). Dream thoughts originating in the unconscious are ordinarily incapable of entering preconsciousness owing to the censorship of the conscious ego. To enter the preconscious they transfer their "affect" to, and take cover in, ideas there; conversely, the conscious wish can originate a dream only if it awakens a similar wish in the unconscious that offers it reinforcement. These dream thoughts are "latent" material which the dream work—"an instance of the unconscious working-over of preconscious thought-processes," according to the *Outline*—renders into the "manifest dream." (XXIII, 167) Because dreams serve to pacify both the unconscious (id) and the conscious ego, Freud refers to them in the *Outline* as "a kind of compromise-formation" (XXIII, 170).

The distinction between the latent and the manifest dream had important consequences for Freud's general psychology because it led to the discovery and enumeration of unconscious processes. It is the manifest dream that the sleeper remembers on waking, and its interpretation discloses those processes—displacement of affect, condensation, and the like—basic to the primary process. Thus the seemingly illogical structure of the dream (illogical to the secondary process or waking thought) has a logic and a wholly consistent meaning of its own: an idea may be represented through its contrary, reflecting the phenomenon of antithetical words in ancient languages (discussed in an essay of 1910); or ordinary logical connections may be expressed through showing events to be simultaneous. In general, ideas are "represented" in concrete pictorial language. Finally, dreams have many meanings, for they represent a series of layered wish fulfillments, "the bottom one being the fulfillment of a wish dating from earliest childhood" (IV, 219) and from the "archaic heritage" of the mind (XXIII, 167).

"The whole thing is planned on the model of an imaginary walk," Freud wrote Fliess in August, 1899:

First comes the dark wood of the authorities (who cannot see the trees), where there is no clear view and it is easy to go astray. Then there is a cavernous defile through which I lead my readers—my specimen dream with its peculiarities, its details, its indiscretions and its bad jokes—and then, all at once, the high ground and the open prospect and the question: "Which way do you want to go?" (IV, 122)

With attention to this statement, one critic has stressed the involuntary revelation that Freud made in the book.[1] The letters to Fliess show that the book helped him in a therapeutic way, but what may seem involuntary is perhaps the result or effect of a rhetoric that seeks to involve the reader in the very act of discovery.

Aware that he was presenting an epochal view of the mind and that the voluminous corpus of writings on dream theory would stand in the way of acceptance of his own view, Freud reviews the most influential ideas and exposes their shortcomings, at the same time suggesting how they could be incorporated into a more penetrating theory. The argument is built inductively, from example to idea, from the more obvious considerations to the less obvious and theoretical, the final theoretical chapter summarizing key ideas and developing the fundamental distinction between the primary and secondary process. The intellectual structure of the argument is, however, dialectical; that is, Freud explores the possibilities of ideas as he proceeds. "We have often seen that in unconscious thinking itself," he states, "every train of thought is yoked with its contradictory opposite" (V, 468). If discursive thought is a secondary activity, guided by the "pleasure principle," and not the product of a separate rational faculty (as *Dreams* would show), the subjective presence of the scientist would not be merely an amiable intrusion into the work.

Freud supplemented clinical observations, on which his previous papers, reports, and encyclopedia articles depended, with materials drawn from his self-analysis. This new resource had a momentous effect on his writing, for it brought the play of imagination and wit to the psychological materials of the essay. The 1899 essay "Screen Memories" shows that Freud was willing and able to disguise his presence and experiment with new "voices." Though drawing on his self-analysis, he identifies the source of an important screen memory only as "someone who is not at all or only very slightly neurotic," and, disguising the facts of his neurosis, adds that the patient "has taken an interest in psychological questions ever since I was able to relieve him of a slight phobia by means of psychoanalysis" (III, 309).[2] The voice here is probably more playful than ironic.

Problems relating to the extensive use of personal materials were clearly on Freud's mind, as the preface to the first edition indicates:

But if I was to report my own dreams, it inevitably followed that I should have to reveal to the public gaze more of the intimacies of my mental life than I liked, or than is normally necessary for any writer who is a man of science and not a poet. (IV, xxiii–iv)

His solution was to omit details which bore chiefly on sexual matters, with the result that the value of his examples was "very definitely diminished" (xxiv). His statement to Fliess that the "involved sentences . . . bolstered up on indirect phrases and with sidelong glances at their subject-matter, have gravely affronted some ideal within me" (xx) shows that his reticence was not feigned. A more open revelation would have better satisfied scientific candor.

There was a gain, however, in these omissions, as there had been in the *Studies*. In the course of the book Freud refers to Schiller's statement that creative writing is hindered if reason looks too closely at ideas that pour in, particularly those of a transient and extravagant quality (IV, 103). If there was to be no total candor in the reporting of his own dreams, there was to be a free flow of ideas and uninhibited revelation of his "private character" (V, 453). As if to compensate for what had been omitted, Freud is candid about his early failures in experimenting with cocaine and sulphonal, his indirect responsibility for the illness and death of a patient and a friend, and his hostility toward medical colleagues who had rejected his ideas on hysteria. He discusses his wish for promotion to a professorship, his sensitivity to anti-Semitism, problems with urination in childhood, his ambivalent feelings toward his father, his fear of ridicule. A recurring theme is his ambition and sense of personal destiny: he mentions his admiration of Hannibal and other world conquerors and reports a prophecy that his mother's first-born would become a great man.

How uninhibited this personal revelation could be is seen in his analysis of a dream in which, like Hercules cleansing the Augean stables, he urinated on a long seat in a privy. He was reminded of how much his patients honored him:

Indeed, even the museum of human excrement could be given an interpretation to rejoice my heart. . . . The stream of urine which washed everything clean was an unmistakable sign of greatness. It was in that way that Gulliver extinguished the great fire in Lilliput. . . . (V, 469)

He was reminded, too, of Gargantua urinating upon Paris from

Notre Dame. The dream originated, he indicates, at a lecture he delivered. A member of the audience

> began to flatter me; telling me how much he had learnt from me, how he looked at everything now with fresh eyes, how I had cleansed the *Augean stables* of errors and prejudices in my theory of the neuroses. He told me, in short, that I was a very great man. My mood fitted ill with the paean of praise; I fought against my feeling of disgust. . . . (V, 470)

Freud concludes that the form of the dream expressed two contradictory states of mind—megalomania and "delusions of inferiority" (V, 470).

As if to heighten the dramatic character of this sort of revelation, Freud returns to motifs of dreams analyzed in earlier pages. For example, the analysis of an important dream involving Fliess and another friend is continued in a later discussion of affects in dreams; it is in this discussion that Freud states that all of his friends have been "reincarnations" of a nephew who had been his close friend in youth. Referring to his emotional need of "an intimate friend and a hated enemy," he concludes that "the ideal situation of childhood has been so completely reproduced that friend and enemy have come together in a single individual —though not, of course, both at once or with constant oscillations" (V, 483).

The dependence on analogy and other figurative devices analyzed by Hyman opened the way to the representation of instinctual trends as imperative forces. His statement that we regain the paradise of childhood in our dreams is merely parabolic, yet the idea increasingly takes on the status of imperative fact as Freud found himself able to deal with psychological ideas free of the restriction of physiological theory, and as these ideas could be fitted into a theory of culture. Thus he applies the idea of the paradise of dreams literally to poetry. The "deepest and eternal nature of man" which the poet evokes is rooted in "a childhood that has since become prehistoric" (IV, 247). A related and important idea is that thinking is "a substitute for a hallucinatory wish" (V, 567). Freud was to make more of this idea in the 1914 essay on narcissism. Commenting that the self-reproaches of conscience coincide with the perceptions on which these reproaches are founded, he comments that the activity of the mind which has taken over the function of conscience has also placed itself at the service of internal research, which furnishes philosophy with the material for its intellectual operations. This may have some bearing on the characteristic tendency of paranoics to construct speculative systems. (XIV, 96)

It is, in fact, primary thinking that is the chief theme of the book. As Ricoeur has indicated, the thrust of the analysis is to establish the primacy of primary thinking and "to give a schematic picture of the descending degrees of desire all the way to the *indestructible.*" There is, by contrast, little consideration of the secondary process.[3] Freud's rhetoric is expended in establishing the primacy and power of those "prehistoric" impulses that are the nucleus of the unconscious. And throughout the book he does not allow the reader to forget that behind the operations of the dream work is the mysterious human personality, of which he is himself the exemplar. He is, in effect, Oedipus answering the riddle of the Sphinx, and he dramatizes that encounter through the book itself. Freud thus projects an image of man in confrontation with irreconcilable and mysterious forces, and he does so by surpassing the objective detail (limited as in the *Studies*) and the objectivity of technical discourse.

II   The Psychopathology of Everyday Life

In a footnote added in 1924, Freud described his book on parapraxes as popular in nature, intending through a series of examples to prove without a theoretical discussion that unconscious mental processes must be assumed (VI, 272). Even in new material added to later editions Freud kept to this intention: his analysis of the mechanisms governing slips of tongue and pen, errors and forgetting, and the like, is brief, and at the end of the book he comments without explanation that parapraxes show that the primary process is operative in our waking life as well as in dreams. He adds that psychoneurotic behavior exhibits these same mechanisms, for there is no clear distinction between normal and abnormal states of mind: "we are all a little neurotic" (VI, 278).

The statement of these ideas in simple language, brilliantly illustrated from clinical experience, continues the advance in style evident in *The Interpretation of Dreams*. Freud recounts how he had promised two books on Venice to a patient who was travelling there against Freud's wishes; one of the books he gave the patient was a study of the Medicis. Recognizing his error, he admitted it at once: "It may, in general, seem astonishing that the urge to tell the truth is so much stronger than is usually supposed. Perhaps, however, my being scarcely able to tell lies any more is a consequence of my occupation with psychoanalysis. As often as I try to distort something I succumb to an error or some other parapraxis that betrays my insincerity" (VI, 221). It is an achievement of style as much as of content that these insights emerge for the reader in much the way Freud reached them himself. As in *Dreams*, narrative is joined with analysis in semifictional modes. And as in his book on *Jokes*, Freud illustrates not only from his own experience but also from his wide reading and his knowledge of Jewish humor and ideas. His interest in linguistic phenomena is evident throughout the book.

The comment just quoted serves a major purpose of the study: to show that "nothing in the mind is arbitrary or undetermined" (VI, 242). Freud was attacking orthodox assumptions about the nature of man. The structure of the argument reveals this clearly: beginning with ordinary experiences and moving to such phenomena as self-injury that stops short of actual suicide (a compromise between the instinct to self-destruction and forces in the world that oppose it), he concludes with comments on determinism and superstition.

Though he does not mount an attack on religious ideas as he would do later, he leads the reader to the view that what is not explained by conscious motivation is explained by the unconscious: there is no "gap" in the life of the mind once we understand this fact (VI, 254). And he states, in discussing superstition and paranoia, that much of the "mythological view" promoted by religion is the projection of "psychology" into the world (VI, 258). To mount a critique of the Christian-bourgeois view of man, which he believed was at the root of opposition to radical scientific progress such as psychoanalysis fostered, he would have to establish, in Ferenczi's phrase, "the animal nature of the unconscious" (VI, 20). The undramatic narrative and Freud's connecting commentary undoubtedly blunted the impact of these conclusions for most readers.

Psychopathology exhibits a powerful quality of Freud's thinking that we have noted frequently: a recognition of the importance of generalizing discoveries. It is worth commenting in more detail on this recognition here, for it is a mistaken view that most or all experimental scientists do recognize this importance. Hans Selye points out that taking notice of a phenomenon is not "discovery" until that phenomenon has been generalized sufficiently to serve as a fruitful hypothesis and increase our understanding of other phenomena and processes: Banting "discovered" insulin as a treatment for diabetes, not a rival, Marcel Gley, who had performed similar experiments seventeen years earlier and described them in sealed notes deposited with the Société de Biologie. Gley had "seen" but had not "discovered" insulin.[4] The distinction is worth noting, given the numerous claims that the unconscious and related ideas were known before Freud. The French psychologist Pierre Janet had made a claim to the discovery of psychoanalysis; in the course of his critique of Janet's views in the autobiographical study, Freud applies the conception of discovery suggested by Selye: "Janet's works would never have had the implications which have made psychoanalysis of such importance to the mental sciences and have made it attract such universal interest" (XX, 20, 31). In other words, Freud not only announced his discovery of the unconscious and associated it with repression: he derived wholly new and unexpected conclusions about its functioning. "Insight such as this falls to one's lot but once in a lifetime," he stated in the Third English Edition of *Dreams* (IV, xxxii).

III   Three Essays on the Theory of Sexuality

Though Freud wrote forcefully on sexual hypocrisy and masturbation in his essay of 1898, "Sexuality in the Aetiology of the Neuroses," his treatment of sexual topics before 1905 tended to be cautious and restrained. Perhaps the added confidence gained through a widening circle of followers changed his attitude, for in the *Three Essays* (and the "Dora" analysis) he was prepared to present his ideas frankly and aggressively: "So far as I know, not a single author has clearly recognized the regular existence of a sexual instinct in childhood," he wrote (VII, 173). The tone of this statement is typical of much of his writing from this time on. It should be added that the book as we have it today contains ideas incorporated into successive editions—additions notably on the child's researches into sexuality, the castration complex, and the phases of sexual organization—and these were put to use as polemics against opponents of the theory of infantile sexuality proposed.

It was undoubtedly the break with Adler and Jung that led to Freud's concern with enlarging his frame of discourse. The preface to the fourth edition of 1920 comments on the "stretching" of the idea of sexuality into unsuspected areas of behavior and reminds the reader "how closely the enlarged sexuality of psychoanalysis coincides with the Eros of the divine Plato" (VII, 134). But the search for correspondences in human and cultural experience is apparent earlier, and Stekel's theory of symbolism (incorporated into *Dreams*) and Jung's and Rank's investigations into mythology and art before 1913 strengthened this concern. The enlargement of the frame of discourse in the *Essays* is achieved through a search for similarities in human behavior—for what was typical in men and women and their culture—and for definitions that would incorporate these similarities into a theory of culture.

All of Freud's writings on sexuality from 1905 on reveal this concern. The 1908 essay on childhood theories emphasizes the consequences of ignorance and sexual hypocrisy, in examples like that of the bewildered bride who thought her husband was urinating into her during sexual intercourse (IX, 224). In the *Essays* Freud prepares for a theory of culture by challenging ordinary concepts of "normality" and seeking thereby to free language from misleading connotations. Thus, in the course of an exhaustive examination in the first essay into sexual aberrations, he reminds his reader that "perverse" behavior is normal in every human being, or at least plays a part in normal sexual behavior, which he explains is constituted of diverse trends not widely understood. It is a mistake, then, to use "perversion" as a term of judgment (VII, 160). It is important also to divorce "inversion" from the notion of "degeneracy," for there is no psychoanalytic evidence to distinguish homosexuals as a group distinct in character; and indeed homosexual feeling is encountered in all neuroses (VII, 138, 166). "Normal" social behavior is consistent with abnormal sexual habits, though the latter are always in the "background" of abnormal social behavior (VII, 161). Comments such as these are scattered throughout the book, and though they do not shape the argument, they do influence the use of language.

To state this point in another way, there is an increasing tendency to choose terms that offer the possibility of "extension." Freud's discussion of masculine and feminine characters in the first essay provides a significant example. In the 1915 edition Freud states:

We should rather be inclined to connect the simultaneous presence of these opposites [sadism and masochism] with the opposing masculinity and femininity which are combined in bisexuality—a contrast *whose significance is reduced in psychoanalysis to that between activity and passivity*. (VII, 160, italics mine)

In the 1924 edition the italicized words were altered to:

which often has to be replaced in psychoanalysis by that between activity and passivity

—clearly a gain in generality since the new formulation does not exclude or "reduce" the original opposition between masculinity and femininity. The whole discussion reveals an assumption pervasive in Freud: that traits will be encountered as "pairs of opposites"—Freud's characterization of sadism and masochism (VII, 160). This is perhaps why he is careful to keep his semantic categories as open as possible.

The flexibility of the terms cited is best illustrated by the 1908 essay "Hysterical Phantasies and Their Relation to Bisexuality," concerned mainly with the role of unconscious phantasy in the formation of hysterical symptoms. Phantasies, Freud states, may originate in the unconscious or in conscious daydreams; if the latter provided satisfaction during masturbation, they become unconscious through repression, and pathogenic if the libido remains unsatisfied or unsublimated. To undo or resolve hysterical symptoms, both a masculine and a feminine phantasy must be uncovered, one of them homosexual. Freud does not refer to active and passive traits in this context, but his comment that the daydreams of women are "invariably" erotic and those of men erotic or ambitious seems to imply such a difference in the popular sense of these words—which is the sense Freud seems to have in mind in the *Essays*. The gain for discussion in the later distinction is that the range of extension is greater. Freud is able through such an extension to show that his theories encompass a range of phenomena either unexplained or (as he shows in additions to the *Essays*) wrongly explained by opponents.[5]

The second and third of the *Essays* (concerning infantile life and puberty) further challenge ordinary views by emphasizing that reality is harsh and unremitting. Not only can children be seduced into becoming "polymorphous perverse"—that is, capable of many kinds of erotic pleasure—they are innately so. Furthermore, growing up means that the child becomes alienated from the deepest sources of personal pleasure, from parents, and perhaps also from the total environment. The dangers and barriers to happiness are immense, for the earliest attachments are the strongest in the life of the child, and excessive parental love may lead to neurosis and emotional and sexual impotence. Equally serious, "premature sexual activity diminishes a child's educability" (VII, 234).

Passages in the *Essays* suggest that many people do escape neurosis, but the weight of the discussion as a whole implies the opposite. Freud was to show in later additions and essays like the 1908 "Character and Anal Erotism" the extensive influence of the pregenital organizations on our lives—frugality, orderliness, and other traits that we consider civilized originate in fixations to these organizations. Freud was in this way attacking the view that the positive goods and values of living are freely and consciously chosen. At the same time, he was not seeking in these essays or later ones to exonerate man from responsibility for his neurotic unhappiness. Unconscious wishes are willed like conscious ones—and will implies responsibility. The language of a comment on Sophocles in the later *Introductory Lectures* is characteristic of how he thought about the matter:

It might easily be supposed that the material of the legend had in view an indictment of the gods and of fate; and in the hands of Euripides, the critic and enemy of the gods, it would probably have become such an indictment. But with the devout Sophocles there is no question of an application of that kind. The difficulty is overcome by the pious sophistry that to bow to the will of the gods is the highest morality even when it promotes crime. (XVI, 331)

To accept that "fate" is a "pious sophistry," but Freud does not state directly why it should be. A comment on the secret power of the *Oedipus* supplies the explanation. The auditor

reacts as though by self-analysis he had recognized the Oedipus complex in himself and had unveiled the will of the gods and the oracle as exalted disguises of his own unconscious. (XVI, 331)

The auditor wills the death of Laius and the marriage to Jocasta in imagination as he observes the play, and he is to carry the moral responsibility for this choice.

The dilemma for mankind is not to be resolved through easy formulas; Freud prefers in the essays of this period to stress the need of insight and exerted effort, as in his comment in the 1908 essay on sexual morality that "indulgence" in masturbation weakens the character; for "it teaches people to achieve important aims without taking trouble and by easy paths instead of through an energetic exertion of force" (IX, 199–200). It is an effort, Freud implies, that must be exerted against society itself. For the price that suppression of instinct and high-mindedness exact is too high; some people would be "more healthy" if they had learned how to be "less good" (IX, 191). Unimpaired sexual experience is desirable, not because it is pleasurable, but because it is therapeutic. And part of the therapy would seem to be resistance to an authority that does not know itself: to a social morality that provides a kind of sexual therapy for the man in countenancing the double standard, but denies it to the woman who is expected to safeguard her virtue at the cost of serious neurotic illness. If happiness is preferable to neurosis, then man and woman must take the responsibility for their own therapy, though Freud does not directly state how this therapy is best achieved. "Psychoanalysis is a therapy for the healthy," Rieff states, "not a solution for the sick—except so far as the sick themselves become analysts, and find in this therapeutic their personal solution, as Freud did."[6]

IV   *"Family Romances" and Essays on the Psychology of Love*

Freud's essays have been praised for their concision of statement and felicitous handling of difficult ideas; but they have also been attacked for vagueness or a looseness of definition and phrasing that makes translation of the original German notoriously difficult. Jones states that "Freud was seldom meticulous in adhering to precise definitions."[7] I have been suggesting that the explanation is to be found not in a habit of mind or a dislike of scientific exactitude but in the desire for concepts, even those of a popular nature, that would permit a broader generalizing of psychoanalytic ideas.

The language and formulations of certain later essays like "Family Romances" show this tendency clearly. So important has this essay been to psychoanalytic literary criticism that its main ideas are worth summarizing in detail. Freud distinguishes the "family romance"—an important phantasy of childhood and later years—through its phases: first, preliminary childhood phantasies in which substitute parents replace the real ones when they provoke hostility; then the first stage of the "neurotic's family romance," occurring before puberty, in which the child substitutes for the real parents ones of higher birth he has actually encountered; finally, the second stage, occurring at puberty and afterwards, in which substitution continues to be made for the father, since his identity can never be verified, but no longer can be made for the mother. These later phantasies are sexual, the child wishing now to observe his mother in secret love affairs, as in certain rescue phantasies (discussed in the first essay on the psychology of love), in which the child is himself the lover of the unfaithful mother whom he seeks to protect from her own weaknesses of character (XI, 171). Motives of revenge are present particularly toward the father, though Freud adds that this hostility is not as deep as it may seem, for the "family romance" (and the rescue phantasy too) also preserves affectionate feelings of an earlier time of life:

Indeed the whole effort at replacing the real father by a superior one is only an expression of the child's longing for the happy, vanished days when his father seemed to him the noblest and strongest of men and his mother the dearest and loveliest of women. He is turning away from the father whom he knows today to the father in whom he believed in the earlier years of his childhood; and his phantasy is no more than the expression of a regret that those happy days have gone. (IX, 240–41)

In a related phantasy, the child returns to the family home to legitimize himself and bastardize his brothers and sisters. In the later essay on the psychology of love, Freud indicates that the father may be the object of a "defiant" rescue phantasy in which the child pays back all that the father has given him. In rescue phantasies in general tenderness and defiance combine in the child's wish "to be his own father" (XI, 173).

Written as an introduction to Rank's *The Myth of the Hero*, "Family Romances" describes these phenomena in the most general terms. And this level of generality of maintained in the "Three Contributions to the Psychology of Love" (1910, 1912, 1918), which Freud originally intended as chapters in an uncompleted work.

The first of these essays concerns the need of some men to debase a woman as a condition of loving her, and as a second condition injuring a "third party" to whom the woman is already attached. In loving this woman, the man is rescuing her—that is, preventing her from sinking even lower than he imagines her to be. Freud's explanation for this behavior, as in rescue phantasies, is that the third person is a surrogate of the father; the woman, a surrogate of the mother. This kind of object choice is thus a remnant of the Oedipus complex (so named for the first time in this essay).

The second of the essays deals further with this tendency to debasement—through analysis of psychical impotence. The cause of this malady is the failure of the affectionate and sensual currents to unite into normal love owing to an unmastered Oedipus complex: "The whole sphere of love in such people remains divided in the two directions personified in art as sacred and profane (or animal) love. Where they love they do not desire and where they desire they cannot love" (XI, 183). Few cultured individuals succeed in uniting the two currents. An increase in sexual freedom is not, however, the solution: "It can easily be shown that the psychical value of erotic needs is reduced as soon as their satisfaction becomes easy" (XI, 187).

The third essay concerns the taboo of virginity. Freud traces primitive defloration rites that employ substitute husbands to the need for directing aroused hostile impulses away from the true husband. The absence of a comparable rite in civilized marriage explains perhaps why first marriages are so often unhappy and why second marriages often succeed so well.

The tension of attitudes in the essay on "civilized" sexual morality (discussed earlier) is maintained in a contemplative irony that intensifies in these essays of the second decade—an irony used to explore the impasse between the individual and his culture that Freud had implied in the 1908 essay. Increasingly, as we suggested, a new pair of opposites absorbs the intellectual tensions earlier invested in the contrast between conscious and unconscious processes: the individual and his enemy, civilization.

Thus we may perhaps be forced to become reconciled to the idea that it is quite impossible to adjust the claims of the sexual instinct to the demands of civilization; that in consequence of its cultural development renunciation and suffering, as well as the danger of extinction in the remotest future, cannot be avoided by the human race. (XI, 190)

Civilization long ago chose the path of repression, and in *Totem and Taboo* Freud indicates when it did and how.

The opening phrase of the passage just quoted is symptomatic of an attitude we also noted earlier: the responsibility of the individual for his unhappiness. As the heir of the "primal horde" and its act of original murder, he must atone to his conscience. The act of atonement is one of acceptance—reconcilement—with the reality of human nature. For there is something in human nature beyond control—"something in the nature of the sexual instinct itself is unfavorable to the realization of complete satisfaction." And Freud varies a statement of Napoleon: "Anatomy is destiny" (XI, 188–89).

The frame of reference is now cultural. Ideas are stated in a philosophical language different from that of the *Essays*. That language is apparent even in a technical essay of the period, "The Two Principles of Mental Functioning" (1911), which introduces the term "pleasure principle," though the concept had been stated in different words and as the "unpleasure principle" earlier. In tracing such mental functions as attention, phantasy, and thinking itself to reality testing, technical language gives way to simile: thinking is "an experimental kind of acting" (XII, 221), designed to make possible toleration of increasing tensions and to delay their discharge (thinking became conscious only when it became attached to verbal residues, Freud indicates). Phrases and distinctions such as this prepare for an increasingly philosophical definition of reality, in this essay briefly indicated through reference to a statement of Shaw's Don Juan that suggests Freud's own pleasure and reality ego (XII, 223). In Shaw's play, Don Juan is the creature of an external Life Force that uses the individual to its own ends. This is exactly the conception that Freud has in mind, even though functions are not really synonymous with forces and the formulations of the essay are intended as heuristic. The earlier mechanistic language that lingered after the "Project" is now almost entirely abandoned for a genetic account which hypostatizes the two "principles" as if they were forces developing independently in the mind of the race.

V *Essays on Narcissism and Metapsychology*

This new direction in his thinking is evident in Freud's statement, at the beginning of the 1914 essay on narcissism, that the situation in psychoanalysis was comparable to that in modern physics. Empirical science "will not envy speculation its privilege of having a smooth, logically unassailable foundation, but will gladly content itself with nebulous, scarcely imaginable basic concepts, which it hopes to apprehend more clearly in the course of its development, or which it is even prepared to replace by others" (XIV, 77). These concepts are the "top" of a structure founded on observation and therefore can be changed or dropped without harm.

But though Freud was drawing into a single theory empirical observations made over a number of years, the essay chiefly seeks to refine terms and at the same time establish a general mode of discourse appropriate to new interests. Thus his answer to Jung's criticism of his reasoning in the Schreber case concerns the ineptness of an analogy Jung employs. But he does not dismiss the possibility of a general libido such as Jung was proposing. The consideration, Freud states, is actually one of relevance:

It may turn out that, most basically and on the longest view, sexual energy—libido—is only the product of a differentiation in the energy at work generally in the mind. But such an assertion has no relevance. It relates to matters which are so remote from the problems of our observation, and of which we have so little cognizance, that it is as idle to dispute it as to affirm it. . . . (XIV, 79)

He wished to see what "a synthesis of the *psychological*

phenomena" would show about an essentially biological problem. The frame of reference of terms employed is thus a central consideration.

The penetrating discussion that follows (the main ideas of which we have considered) leads to a series of generalizations in which technical distinctions, whose extensions Freud had severely limited in the statement quoted, are applied without qualification. For example, he uses his analysis to explain the great attraction of narcissistic women, criminals, and humorists in literature as resulting from their "unassailable libidinal position" which most people have given up. A succeeding comment on the erotic life of narcissistic women suggests that the frame of reference in this discussion is actually indeterminate:

> . . . I know that these different lines of development correspond to the differentiation of functions in a highly complicated biological whole; further, I am ready to admit that there are quite a number of women who love according to the masculine type and who also develop the sexual overvaluation proper to that type. (XIV, 89)

Such considerations are, however, subordinate to conclusions Freud was able to draw. To have established correspondences in this way is to have treated terms as metaphors—in the phrase of Wallace Stevens, to have made things "brilliant."

The five essays that comprise the "torso" of a metapsychology were theoretical bridges to the later instinctual theory. "I broke off, wisely perhaps," Freud states in his autobiography, "since the time for theoretical predications of this kind had not yet come" (XX, 59). "Instincts and Their Vicissitudes," "Repression," and "The Unconscious" appeared in 1915; the supplement to the dream theory discussed earlier, and "Mourning and Melancholia," did not appear until 1917. The first three essays are almost purely technical and aim to systematize the various lines of thought pursued in the later theoretical chapters of *Dreams* and other essays of the first decade.

Freud is chiefly concerned with unifying concepts in semantic categories in which psychological distinctions would be at least consistent with biological investigation and could meet the test of scientific exactitude in the process of generalization. Thus in the first of the essays he identifies three polarities of mental life, each an antithesis: ego and object (the external world), pleasure and unpleasure, active and passive, coalescing later with masculine and feminine. He applies these distinctions in a characteristic way to the phenomenon of love, which he traces through its various stages, indicating that it becomes the opposite of hate (deriving from the ego's narcissistic rejection of the world at the time the genital organization is complete). In "Repression" he distinguishes between "primal repression"—the denial to consciousness of the "ideational" representative of an instinct—and "repression proper," in which derivatives or ideas associated with the repressed content experience an "after-pressure." The tendency to repression comes from the working together of these forces. Then follows a dramatization of repression, designed to illuminate the feelings of the neurotic: "It proliferates in the dark, as it were, and takes on extreme forms of expression, which when they are translated and presented to the neurotic are not only bound to seem alien to him, but frighten him by giving him the picture of an extraordinary and dangerous strength of instinct" (XIV, 149).

The long technical essay on the unconscious emphasizes that only the "ideational" representative of an instinct can become conscious, and it distinguishes between the conscious and unconscious on the basis of an idea developed in different language earlier: they are not "different registrations" of the same material in different locations in the mind, nor "different functional states of cathexis" in the same location, "but the conscious presentation comprises the presentation of the thing plus the presentation of the word belonging to it, while the unconscious presentation is the presentation of the thing alone" (XIV, 201). The semantic problem is central here. The emphasis is now on the discovery of the unconscious through verbal residues—a functional process. The passage illustrates the process of translation by which spatial or topographical characterizations of the unconscious (with stress on static, "eternal" features) became dynamic ones (with stress on the aims of instincts). He had stated in "Instincts and Their Vicissitudes":

Although instincts are wholly determined by their origin in a somatic source, in mental life we know them only by their aims. An exact knowledge of the sources of an instinct is not invariably necessary for purposes of psychological investigation; sometimes its source may be inferred from its aim. (XIV, 123)

Running through these three essays is a basic theme:

psychological reality can be known, though as the passage just quoted suggests not directly or exactly. Freud had of course devoted many pages to the possibility of this knowledge earlier, but he had not dealt with the question philosophically. It is significant, then, that in these technical discussions he deals briefly with the epistemological implications of his views. The psychoanalytic unconscious, he states, seems to be an "expansion of the primitive animism which caused us to see copies of our own consciousness all around us" and also an "extension" of Kant's critique of "external perception" (XIV, 171). Freud means that the demonstration of the systematic difference between consciousness and the unconscious gives weight (though not proof) to Kant's separation between "subjectively conditioned" perception and "what is perceived though unknowable." The unexpected discovery made possible by psychoanalysis is that "internal objects are less unknowable than the external world."[8]

This discussion (occurring at the end of the first part of "The Unconscious") helps to explain why the original and unsatisfactory concept of the unconscious was not discarded following the statement of the structural hypothesis in the 1920's: the concept was a guarantee of the claim of psychoanalysis to *scientific* importance—not philosophical. For philosophical inquiry, Freud seems to have believed, is mainly unfinished business, the indispensable predecessor to genuine scientific advancements—which are advances in *definition*, in increasingly exact formulations (XIV, 177). It is not coincidental that he opens "Instincts and Their Vicissitudes" with an inquiry into the relation between hypothesis, definition, and empirical observation: "Even at the stage of description it is not possible to avoid applying certain abstract ideas to the material in hand, ideas derived from somewhere or other but certainly not from the new observations alone" (XIV, 117). The statement is an advance over that quoted from the earlier essay on narcissism. Science, like the psychoanalytic session itself, is a discourse—a dialectical mode of discovery joined to empirical investigation.

"Mourning and Melancholia" is an outstanding example of this kind of discourse and surely one of Freud's greatest pieces of writing. The limited clinical evidence on melancholia made it necessary for him to work with abstract ideas chiefly. The focus of the essay is melancholia, a pathological disorder sharing the traits of mourning, including disinterest in the external world and severe dejection. Peculiar to melancholia is the self-abasement of the mourner. In mourning the world has been impoverished by loss of the loved one, but no element of the loss is unconscious; in melancholia the ego itself feels impoverished, and some part of the experience of loss is unconscious. The self-abasement of the melancholic provides the explanation for this difference: the qualities condemned in oneself are actually those displaced from the lost love object. This love object was originally chosen narcissistically and later caused pain and disappointment. Instead of making a new attachment, the libido turned back into the ego, where through a cleavage or split one part of the ego identified with the lost love object while the other attacked or reproached it for the pain caused (XIV, 249). Freud applies this highly subtle and deductive analysis to the phenomenon of suicide: the ego can destroy itself because it deals with itself as an object and makes use of its original hostility toward the world. It is strengthened in this resolve by sadism to which the ego has regressed in its ambivalence.

The abbreviated style of the previous essays gives way now to highly pointed sentences that rise to an eloquent summing up:

[The patient] also seems to us justified in certain other self-accusations; it is merely that he has a keener eye for the truth than other people who are not melancholic. When in his heightened self-criticism he describes himself as petty, egoistic, dishonest, lacking in independence, one whose sole aim has been to hide the weaknesses of his own nature, it may be, so far as we know, that he has come pretty near to understanding himself; we only wonder why a man has to be ill before he can be accessible to a truth of this kind. (XIV, 246)

The melancholic is in this way imagined, and Freud brings to his situation his new awareness of powerful narcissistic behavior. Instincts are now consistently expressed as forces whose objects may correspond to internal, introjected ones. Theory and language are now flexible and abstract—and able to show the way to more adventurous exploration.

VI   Introductory Lectures on Psychoanalysis

His practice having fallen off during the war, Freud was able to give time to a general review of twenty or more years of thought;

the first set of introductory lectures (delivered in the winters of 1915–16 and 1916–17) was the result. Though he largely restated ideas of earlier books and essays, he also developed in more detail his views on dream symbolism and analytic procedure and presented new ideas on primal phantasies and anxiety. These lectures were Freud's first extended integral account of psychoanalysis (his five lectures at Clark University in 1909 are concerned with fewer topics), and they provided the first introduction to psychoanalysis for many (and continue to do so).

To those knowing little or nothing of the history of the libido theory, some of the discussion may be perplexing; for in the later chapters on symptom formation and narcissism Freud's terminology derives from his recent thinking on narcissism. Indeed, he was rethinking the nature of anxiety, so that inordinate attention is given to ideas that were shortly to undergo drastic revision. Thus he refers to the superego without naming it (in "Mourning and Melancholia" he anticipated the concept in distinguishing functions of the ego), but the still central distinction between conscious and unconscious layers of the mind organizes the discussion. In the essay on narcissism Freud suggested that the ego instincts might also be libidinal through their original attachment to the sexual instincts. In an effort to preserve his assumption that the instincts were dual, he now attributed two kinds of energy to the ego instincts: "ego interest," the distinctive self-preserving energy of the ego, and the narcissistic libido that he had shown to be transformable into object-libido (XVI, 414–15). Three years later, in *Beyond the Pleasure Principle*, he was to give up this distinction and state that the two kinds of energy were one and the same. His continuing awareness of the challenge presented by Jung is evident in his statement that "the name of libido is properly reserved for the instinctual forces of sexual life, as has hitherto been our practice" (XVI, 413).

Perhaps no work of Freud's more reveals the complexity of his attitude toward psychoanalysis, and never had he been more outspoken about its importance. Beginning with a survey of the obstacles to its general acceptance—the fears aroused by his frankness about sexuality in a society anxious not to be reminded "of this precarious portion of its foundations" (XV, 23), the intimate talk central to psychotherapy and the problem of transference, the demand of truthfulness that psychoanalysis enforces on the patient—Freud moves to what may be the most serious obstacle of all, the challenge of psychoanalysis to the mistaken assumption of "psychical freedom" (XV, 49). Throughout the lectures he returns to deliver a blow to this assumption: he calls attention to the "determinism whose rule extends over mental life" (XV, 106) and to the peculiar rationality and coherence of unconscious life (XV, 226). He also suggests that neurosis is grounded in "a kind of ignorance—a not knowing about mental events that one ought to know of" (XVI, 280).

That his rationalist premises might not be compatible with the knowledge gained in clinical practice is an implied concern of the later lectures, and Freud deals with this concern semantically. Thus the view of neurosis just quoted seemed to him an approximation of Socratic ideas, which assume that vice is grounded in ignorance. He admits, however, that "Knowledge is not always the same as knowledge" (XVI, 281), for the doctor's cannot become the patient's without the phenomenon of transference. Still "our thesis that the symptoms vanish when their sense is known remains true in spite of this."

But was understanding the sufficient condition of the virtuous life, and was virtue itself a rational idea? Freud was certain only that the answer was not to be found in the thinking of society about morality: "We tell ourselves that anyone who has succeeded in educating himself to truth about himself is permanently defended against the danger of immorality, even though his standard of morality may differ in some respect from that which is customary in society" (XVI, 434). Society cannot say what are rational sexual practices, nor is sexual liberation the alternative (a theme of the essays on the psychology of love). This recognition is an important source of Freud's pessimism. Another is that neurosis may be the basis of mankind's "prerogative" over animals. Neurosis is the price of "a richly articulated mental life," the "reverse side" of man's considerable endowments (XVI, 414).

Toward the end of the lectures he summarizes a truth he had enunciated in so many different contexts earlier:

A recommendation to the patient to "live a full life" sexually could not possibly play a part in analytic therapy—if only because we ourselves have declared that an obstinate conflict is taking place in him between a libidinal impulse and sexual repression, between a sensual and an ascetic trend. (XVI, 432–33)

But he had not yet uncovered the cause of this seemingly intractable situation: the answer lay ahead in the revision of the dual instinctual theory. The note of philosophical anxiety in these pages indicates that Freud felt his most important formulations lay ahead.

CHAPTER 5

Freud's Theory of Literature

I Art as Neurosis

"THE subjective determinants of the joke-work," Freud states in his 1905 book on wit, "are often not far removed from those of neurotic illness" (VIII, 142). Since art is associated with play in his thinking, the association with neurosis seems a contradiction; but play is itself a complex phenomenon, not to be confused with trivial activity: "The opposite of play is not what is serious but what is real," he states in the 1908 essay "Creative Writers and Daydreaming." Play is as "serious" as the "real" because it is the manifestation of unconscious forces. It is a form of fantasizing: "The creative writer does the same as the child at play. He creates a world of phantasy which he takes very seriously—that is, which he invests with large amounts of emotion—while separating it sharply from reality" (IX, 144). It is this separation that connects art with neurosis.

Freud did adopt in other passages a much less serious stance toward play, one farther removed from neurotic traits in being a euphoric, essentially free play of the faculties for their own sake.[1] The more serious conception, by contrast, stresses two rather different purposes: the maintenance of mental equilibrium (one concern of the 1905 book), and the cathartic function of art in resolving psychical conflict, an implied concern that came to dominate Freud's theory. One aim of the 1905 book, as we shall see, was to find a place for "euphoric" activity—the free play of the faculties—in the conception of art as catharsis.

The increasing stress on art as catharsis led Freud to a conception that was also rhetorical, since the "essential *ars poetica*" consists in "overcoming the feeling of repulsion in us which is un-doubtedly connected with the barriers that rise between each single ego and the others" (IX, 153). In this conception the artist—unlike the dreamer but like the maker of jokes—seeks to make himself intelligible to others. Whereas dreams "communi-cate" nothing and as a compromise between internal forces re-main "unintelligible" to the dreamer and are therefore of no in-terest to others, the joke is the "most social" of mental functions that seek pleasure: "It often calls for three persons and its com-pletion requires the participation of someone else in the mental process it starts." It must therefore be intelligible, and to this end employs the distortions of unconscious processes "up to the point at which it can be set straight by the third person's under-standing" (VIII, 179).

But the process of communication is potentially full of conflict. So dangerous is the content of self-centered daydreams or phan-tasies that form the work of art that the artist must bribe his au-dience with a "purely formal" or "esthetic" pleasure—an "incen-tive bonus" or "fore-pleasure," Freud indicates in *Three Essays* (IX, 153). The use of "fore-pleasure" as a characterization suggests the regressive quality of the experience. This quality is particu-larly evident in the obscene joke—strongly sadistic and therefore deriving its energy from the infantile organizations—that Freud used as a model for the artistic process.

To explain why the artist often seems exuberant and unrepress-ed, Freud suggests that he is more susceptible to sublimation than is the ordinary man and is able to ease the repressions that provide the content of egoistic daydreaming (XVI, 376). Why the artist should seek the exuberant and euphoric is clear enough; but why he should want to make himself intelligible to others, why art is properly understood as a form of rhetoric—the artistic process conceived as a social activity, the generation and resolu-tion of conflict necessarily involving more than one person—was perhaps not clear to Freud until he was able to understand the artist historically. *Totem and Taboo* and the later *Group Psychology* provided the historical explanation.

We shall consider this explanation in the final chapter, but its main features may be summarized briefly. The epic poet origi-nally created the heroic myth out of longing for the primal father who had been killed by the horde. Indeed, the poet himself is the hero who slew the father: he is the tragic hero. The audience, longing also for the slain father, identifies with the poet. Since the myth is the means by which the individual "emerges from group psychology" (XVIII, 136), art is an achievement of individual feeling, rooted in the historical experience of the race—in conflict and in neurosis itself. Each work of art is a renewal of that achievement: art is both individual and social in motive and significance.

II   Jokes and Their Relation to the Unconscious

At the end of his book on jokes, Freud states that joking, the comic, and humor seek to recover the "euphoria" of childhood when psychical processes operated without their help and with "a small expenditure of energy" (VIII, 236). They are not, however, purely euphoric activities since they derive from economies of various sorts—the comic, from an economy in the energy expended in thinking (as in surprise at seeing someone behave like an automaton); humor, from an economy in feeling (as in the irony which relieves a state of tension); joking, from an economy in "inhibition." Joking is the more complex activity because it draws upon unconscious processes: a preconscious idea is "given over for a moment to unconscious revision" and then made conscious (VIII, 166). The form or "envelope" of the joke—shaped by such primary processes as condensation and displacement—is what makes us laugh. In other words, it is the wording and not the substance that triggers our response; a joke will not be funny if it is "told" in the wrong way. (VIII, 92)

Nevertheless, the substance must be important enough to explain the "inhibition." Considered from this point of view, the joke seems to be cathartic. And indeed the distinction between "innocent" or non-tendentious jokes, which make us smile, and tendentious jokes, which provoke bursts of laughter, would seem to support this interpretation. So potentially dangerous are the energies released in the tendentious joke that we must wonder whether the "envelope" is a way of making the substance acceptable to consciousness. This was exactly how Freud accounted for the "manifest" content of dreams. But the explanation of jokes is different: "For jokes do not, like dreams, create compromises;

they do not evade the inhibition, but they insist on maintaining play with words or with nonsense unaltered" (VIII, 172). This clearly observable difference leads Freud to stress the euphoric: joking as playing with words and thoughts at its simplest. And play is the ostensible motive of the jest, too: "In jests what stands in the foreground is the satisfaction of having made possible what was forbidden by criticism" (VIII, 129). Freud seems to be stressing the same kind of euphoric pleasure in his definition of the joke:

If what a jest says possesses substance and value, it turns into a joke. A thought which would deserve our interest even if it were expressed in the most unpretentious form is now clothed in a form which must give us enjoyment on its own account. (VIII, 131)

The wording of a statement that follows indicates, however, that it is the thought or substance which is really important:

The thought seeks to *wrap itself* in a joke because in that way it recommends itself to our attention and can seem more significant and more valuable, but above all because this *wrapping* bribes our powers of criticism and confuses them. (VIII, 132; italics mine)

The form of the joke, then, is what makes the substance acceptable to consciousness. Throughout this discussion words like "satisfaction" and "enjoyment" remain indeterminate.

The logical difficulty here is that Freud cannot explain how the motive of play is sufficient to evade the "inhibition" or how play is able to do so. He seems to realize the problem in an earlier comment that

the joking activity should not, after all, be described as pointless or aimless, since it has the unmistakable aim of evoking pleasure in its hearers. I doubt if we are in a position to undertake *anything* without having an intention in view.

And he immediately proceeds to a tentative explanation of euphoric play:

If we do not require our mental apparatus at the moment for supplying one of our indispensable satisfactions, we allow it itself to work in the direction of pleasure and we seek to derive pleasure from its own activ-

ity. I suspect that this is in general the condition that governs all aesthet-
ic ideation, but I understand too little of aesthetics to try to enlarge on
this statement. (VIII, 95–96)

Euphoric play may then be a *condition* of the more serious
cathartic activity of the mental apparatus, but, as Freud recog-
nizes, the formulation cannot explain how an idea normally under
repression is able to "evade the inhibition" without being altered
or compromised.

The distinction between the "innocent" joke, which provides
only mild pleasure, and the tendentious joke implies a not very
satisfactory solution: non-tendentious joking is euphoric, tendentious joking cathartic. Freud's concern is chiefly with the second,
and in particular with the obscene joke, on the basis of which he
generalizes on the nature of art.

The purpose of the obscene joke is the arousal of sexual excitement as a substitute for an "act of sexual aggression." It is directed, however, not to the original target but to a person who
laughs at the joke as if he were witnessing the actual seduction
(VIII, 97). This essential "third person" is accounted for by an
alteration in the motive of the aggressor. For when the woman
delays in consenting to the sexual act, the libidinal motive
changes in character and becomes cruel, and the exposure of the
woman—the aim now of the aggressor—is achieved through an
ally. It is this "transformation" that provides the *defining* characteristic of the joke—not the "substance and value" of the joke itself.

Freud may have sought to introduce ideas associated with
euphoric play into this formulation—to show how the free play of
mind might after all enhance the cathartic effect. The presence of
the "third person" necessitates a certain amount of "benevolence"
and "neutrality" (possibly euphoric feelings) to prevent the arousal in the audience of "feelings opposed to the purpose of the
joke" (VIII, 145), and the avoidance of enough intellectual expenditure to erase its effect (VIII, 150).

Freud generalized these special features in commenting on all
types of jokes. Joking is essentially a rhetorical act. The third person must be created in the image of the maker of the joke:

Thus every joke calls for a public of its own and laughing at the same
jokes is evidence of far-reaching psychical conformity. Here moreover we

have arrived at a point which enables us to guess still more precisely what takes place in the third person. He must be able as a matter of habit to erect in himself the same inhibition which the first person's joke has overcome, so that, as soon as he hears the joke, the readiness for this inhibition will compulsively or automatically awaken. (VIII, 151)

It also undoes the repressions which civilization imposes. From the beginning, as I suggested earlier, Freud was convinced of the relation between the joke work and the determinants of neurotic illness. Joking is compulsive activity, not euphoric: the comic can be enjoyed alone, but the joke *"must* be told to someone else" (VIII, 143). And it is the joke that provides the model for the *"ars poetica"* as an overcoming of the sense of repulsion that divides people. Freud might have generalized from the activities of the preconscious comedy and humor, instead of from the joke work, but he was predisposed to identify esthetic experience with the deeper experience of a Hamlet or an Oedipus.

Later formulations were sometimes efforts to reconcile the euphoric and the cathartic. Freud states in "Two Principles of Mental Functioning" that the independent, purposeless play of the pleasure principle—identified as "phantasying" and "day-dreaming" (XII, 222)—is transformed through art into the purposive makebelieve of art, without the necessity of "following the long roundabout path of making real alterations in the external world" (XII, 224). The pleasure principle—the euphoric—is actually being satisfied through the "roundabout path" of the cathartic. In the 1927 essay on humor, this cathartic effect is expressed as comforting. For humor makes traumas occasions of pleasure and rids one of "affects" natural to a situation; it is the "triumph of narcissism, the victorious assertion of the ego's invulnerability" (XXI, 162). Humor, Freud adds, is made possible by the superego which suppresses the reactions of the ego to painful situations. The superego, in short, performs the unaccustomed role of comforting the ego: narcissism is now the expression of the euphoric.

Given these views, Freud was not prepared to make extraordinary claims for the imagination, though his phrasing occasionally suggests Romantic ideas; for example, he comments in "Two Principles of Mental Functioning" on "truths of a new kind," molded from phantasies by the "special gifts" of the artist (XII, 224). His typical view was that the "creative" imagination does not invent: it is capable only of combining diverse experiences, he states in the course of a discussion of the dream work in the *Introductory Lectures* (XV, 172). Nor is the artist concerned with truth per se. Every philosopher and writer "makes his own psychology for himself," he states in *The Question of Lay Analysis* (XX, 192). Commenting on "poetic license" and the need of transformation in the essay "A Special Type of Choice," he suggests that artists show little interest in the "origin and development of the mental states which they portray in their completed form" (XI, 165).

III   Delusions and Dreams in Jensen's *Gradiva*

If the imagination is incapable of inventing, how are the extraordinary insights of creative writers—particularly into processes like dream formation, repression, and "negative hallucination"—to be explained? This important question is the basis of an examination of a short novel by the German writer, Wilhelm Jensen.[2]

The young archaeologist hero of the novel, Norbert Hanold, becomes obsessed with a girl in ancient dress pictured on a basrelief in his possession. The girl he believes was an inhabitant of Pompeii, and one night he dreams of her being destroyed in the eruption of Vesuvius. Later, on a visit to Pompeii, he is amazed to see her come out of a house, looking as she did in his dream. In a series of encounters, Norbert discovers that she is a living person and tells her of his dream and of the girl on the relief. The girl, Zoe, is in fact a forgotten childhood friend, who has been living in a house close to his own, and has been in love with him since childhood. On hearing the details of his phantasies, she realizes that he has suppressed his love for her and through a ruthless interrogation, a kind of "psychical treatment," manages to restore his memory and reawaken his love. At the end of his account, Freud admits that he has treated Norbert and Zoe as "real people and not as the author's creations, as though the author's mind were an absolutely transparent medium and not a refractive or obscuring one" (IX, 41).

Jensen's insights suggest that it is both transparent and refractive; for it copies reality with remarkable fidelity and yet contributes something of its own. Indeed Jensen proves once more that the creative writer is often in advance of scientific discovery, for he was able to show that the "dreamer's erotic longings were stirred up during the night and made a powerful effort to make conscious his memory of the girl he loved and so to tear him out of his delusion," but that this longing was to remain repressed, emerging as anxiety, which explains the death of Gradiva in the destruction of Pompeii (IX, 61). Each detail of the novel has psychological meaning; in fact, Jensen "never introduces a single idle or unintentional feature into his story" (IX, 68). The ambiguities of statement, moreover, are true to the character of dreams and delusions. The modern Gradiva, in restoring Hanold to his memory of her, performs the role of psychotherapist and indeed improves upon the "transference" in her willingness to assume the role of lover and wife (IX, 89–90).

Freud's explanation is that the artist is like the psychotherapist in his insight into unusual mental states. He draws on evidences of these processes in his own mind and expresses them artistically instead of "suppressing them by conscious criticism . . . he need not state these laws, nor even be clearly aware of them; as a result of the tolerance of his intelligence, they are incorporated within his creations" (IX, 92). But Freud had never argued that the psychotherapist need suffer from the delusions and abnormalities of his patients to be able to analyze them, and he does not explain here how the writer is able to describe such an abnormal process as "negative hallucination" unless he was himself the victim of such a disorder.

But here at least was implicit confirmation that the artistic process often originates in neurotic disorder (or states much like it), much as the material which the intellect transforms into philosophy (Freud states in his essay on narcissism) arises in the "internal research" fostered by conscience. "This may have some bearing on the characteristic tendency of paranoics to construct speculative systems," he adds (XIV, 96). An exact formulation of the artistic process was perhaps impossible, for the distinction between normal and pathological states is "conventional," both occurring in the daily lives of every person (IX, 44).

Freud's exploration of phantasy in art, in later essays, reveals his continuing concern with this problem. In "Creative Writers and Daydreaming" he distinguishes many kinds of fantasizing and daydreaming, including the "over-luxuriant and over-powerful" that are a condition of neurosis and psychosis. The modern psychological novelist, he indicates, splits his ego into "many part-egos" and in this way is able "to personify the conflicting currents of his own mental life in several heroes" (IX, 150). Just as he has been aroused by a present experience that reminds him of a childhood one, so is his reader; the work of art thus serves to fulfill wishes and release tensions. In the 1919 essay on the "uncanny," Freud indicates that the writer may keep the reader in a state of uncertainty and create a feeling of the uncanny, by not stating whether "he is taking us into the real world or into a purely fantastic one of his own creation" (XVII, 230).

The creative writer is like the child at play, Freud states in "Creative Writers and Daydreaming." Play and catharsis are in this essay shown to be commensurate experiences, but catharsis is of central importance, for play is conceived as tension-ridden. The statement on the modern psychological novelist quoted above emphasizes conflict in the ego of the writer, not its unity.

The topic is dealt with more profoundly in the earlier "Psychopathic Characters on the Stage," which begins with an explanation of the "purge" or catharsis of emotions in drama:

In this connection the prime factor is unquestionably the process of getting rid of one's own emotions by "blowing off steam"; and the consequent enjoyment corresponds on the one hand to the relief produced by a thorough discharge and on the other hand, no doubt, to an accompanying sexual excitation. . . .

The reader, Freud continues, is like the child for whom play is a compensatory activity, gratifying a wish to act as an adult:

The spectator is a person who experiences too little, who feels that he is a "poor wretch to whom nothing of importance can happen," who has long been obliged to damp down, or rather displace, his ambition to stand in his own person at the hub of world affairs. . . . (VII, 305)

He wishes, in short, to be a hero.

Types of literature may indeed be analyzed through compensatory gratification (the venting of strong feeling in lyric poetry, the identification with the triumphant hero in epic poetry) and arranged hierarchically according to the depth of the emotional needs probed and satisfied. Thus drama offers "masochistic satisfaction" in the defeat of the hero, as well as the "direct enjoyment of a character whose greatness is insisted upon in spite of everything" (VII, 306), and dramas differ according to the ground on which the action producing the suffering is fought. In psychological drama the struggle is in the hero's mind; in drama of character it is between two unbridled heroes for whom social conventions mean little or nothing.

Psychopathological drama, for example *Hamlet*, is perhaps the most complex. The conflict here is between a conscious and a repressed impulse:

> Here the precondition of enjoyment is that the spectator should himself be a neurotic, for it is only such people who can derive pleasure instead of simple aversion from the revelation and the more or less conscious recognition of a repressed impulse. (VII, 308–309)

The person who is not a neurotic will feel only aversion and will seek to maintain the successful repression of the impulse; the neurotic, by contrast, will experience enjoyment but also "resistance." The defining quality of this kind of drama, it should be noted, is the stability of the repression: the neurotic, whose repressions are unstable and require continual expenditures of energy, is spared an expenditure when the repressed impulse is represented, the economy serving as the basis of enjoyment. The form of the drama is analyzed according to this definition. Thus the hero must *become* psychopathic, not be so at the start. The repressed impulse must be common to the hero and audience alike; it must not be named specifically. These preconditions must be kept in mind in constructing the drama, for they permit identification with the hero, not a rejection of him as someone too abnormal to be of interest. "It would seem to be the dramatist's business to induce the same illness in *us*; and this can best be achieved if we are made to follow the development of the illness along with the sufferer" (VII, 310).

If we read these comments in light of the later statements in "Creative Writers and Daydreaming," it would seem that an art based on repressed materials does not require a knowledge of the author's biography for its interpretation. The stipulation that the repressed impulse be shared by author and spectator means that the author is understood to be the spectator or reader of his own

work: we learn about him as we analyze our commensurate responses to it. Reader psychology—the rhetorical consideration
—proves to be the key to the creative imagination.

IV The Methods of Psychobiography

If art and neurosis are so closely joined, what is the explanation
for the sublimated art of a Leonardo da Vinci who seems to have
escaped neurosis? Freud tried to answer this question in his 1910
study of the artist, his first and perhaps most important work in
psychobiography.

The answer he proposes is that the artist may escape neurosis
through sublimation, but this achievement is tenuous and easily
undone. Leonardo originally escaped the first two of the vicissitudes of the "instinct for research" active in infancy: these are
the severe neurotic inhibition that ordinarily restricts intelligence
and creativity and the sexualization of thought that ordinarily
produces severe anxiety and brooding. Leonardo instead achieved
the "rarest and most perfect" vicissitude: the sublimation of libido
acting freely in the service of intellectual curiosity and reinforced
by the original instinct. In this "vicissitude," sexual repression
does occur, but none of the component instincts are made unconscious; neurosis is evaded in this way, but at a price. For sexual
repression is "still taken into account by the instinct, in that it
avoids any concern with sexual themes" (XI, 79–80). The highly
sublimated art of a Leonardo is thus compulsive in its own way.
Thus Freud suggests that in the smiling women of the most famous pictures "Leonardo has denied the unhappiness of his erotic
life, and has triumphed over it in his art, by representing the
wishes of the boy, infatuated with his mother, as fulfilled in this
blissful union of the male and female natures" (XI, 118). He is
referring in this statement to Leonardo's over-fond mother who
Freud believes nurtured, in the crucial years of infancy when she
raised the boy alone, a passive homosexuality that promoted his
highly intellectual, sublimated temperament.

So tenuous was his achievement that neurosis remained a possibility and did, Freud believes, finally become manifest. His
delay in completing pictures like *The Last Supper* suggests that
Leonardo experienced a mental process comparable to neurotic

regression (XI, 133). Owing to the loss of a fatherly patron and to changes in his personal life, the sublimation that had turned Leonardo into an artist at puberty gave way to the original instinct for research: "the almost total repression of a real sexual life does not provide the most favorable conditions for the exercise of sublimated sexual trends" (XI, 133). Gradually Leonardo turned from art to scientific investigation, this new research satisfying different instincts in being rigid and inflexible.

Freud's reasoning throughout this psychobiography is deductive, though the exposition proceeds in inductive fashion, inspired mainly by details in D. S. Merezhkovsky's 1902 novel on Leonardo. The method is deductive because certain assumptions derived from these details and other sources govern the selection of evidence. Freud reasons chiefly from a supposed early memory of Leonardo—recorded in the notebooks and quoted by Merezhkovsky—that a vulture had attacked him in the cradle, striking its tail against his lips. Freud interprets the memory as a later phantasy drawing on early experiences and precipitated by Leonardo's possible discovery of an ancient Egyptian fable that all vultures are female and reproduce without assistance of a male. Leonardo presumably identified his mother with the vulture, assuming, as children normally do, that women possess the male genital.[3] Only the deductive method, it may be noted, permits such conjecture. The two mothers in the *Madonna and Child with St. Anne* are explained by the supposed fact that in his later childhood Leonardo's father brought him into his house; the two women in the picture are Leonardo's stepmother and his father's mother, who continued to lavish their love on him. From their smiles (and from the smile of the *Mona Lisa*) Freud deduces Leonardo's absorption in his early life and art with "the contrast between reserve and seduction, and between the most devoted tenderness and a sensuality that is ruthlessly demanding" (XI, 108).

It may be asked whether the psychobiographer can work in any but a deductive way, for he works indirectly with his subject and must himself select the evidence (contrary to the practice of psychotherapy). The early studies on hysteria and even some of the later case histories are closer to inductive investigations, though in the writing Freud is tracing discoveries and theories already made and formulated. Most of these studies are based, however, on some clinical experience with the subjects. The evidence during actual encounters emerged gradually and slowly assumed systematic proportions. The psychobiographer, on the other hand, comes upon his evidence in another way, and he is likely to choose that evidence which confirms an earlier theory. There is nothing intrinsically "unscientific" about this procedure: the investigator may begin with a choice of hypothesis or problem for research and with a judgment about the relative worth of available evidence. The obvious difficulty is that evidence such as Freud works with in the study of Leonardo is second hand and incapable of verification.

Aware of the indiscretion involved in such procedures, if not of these hazards, Freud tried to solve the problem of evidence by stressing what was typical and ordinary in Leonardo, subject as he was to "laws which govern both normal and pathological activity with equal cogency" (XI, 63). The use of "analogies from primitive times" would give his conclusions the support of general psychoanalytic truths (XI, 96). Freud stresses the mysteriousness of the creative process, but he does so probably because second-hand evidence is dangerous to work with and not because his view of the imagination is Romantic.

Following his lead, psychoanalytic literary critics have focused on distinctive patterns of meaning that can be sufficiently generalized. Biographical details such as may be available are fitted to these patterns (a notable example is Bernard C. Meyer's extraordinary study of Joseph Conrad). The danger of such an approach arises not in the perception of distinctive patterns but in dependence on presumed universal symbols and reductive formulas. So long as the richness of the works is not absorbed into the underlying psychological pattern, the "sameness" often criticized in Freudian studies need not arise. In Freud's best case histories not everything is finished off or resolved—no more than in "interminable" analysis. There are no "cures" (like Leonardo's early sublimations) that could be, or were shown to be, permanent. The psychobiographies are far less successful, perhaps because (as Spector shows in his penetrating analysis of *Leonardo*) Freud had identified too closely with his subject and therefore focused on evidence (and held to it rigorously) that touched upon his own unresolved neurotic situation.

Freud's single venture into political psychobiography—in his co-authorship with William C. Bullitt of a study of Woodrow Wilson (1967)—is a revealing study of the messianic complex, following up ideas briefly treated in the Schreber case. It is, however, more seriously flawed a work than the study of Leonardo exactly because nothing in Wilson is permitted to remain mysterious. Wilson's complex character and actions are explained virtually through a single motive—his repressed aggressiveness toward a father he worshipped all his life—and without supporting evidence. Though the authors admit that the study was based on incomplete evidence and could not therefore be characterized as psychoanalytic, they nevertheless deal with Wilson's aggressiveness categorically.[4] Their main argument is that Wilson dealt with this aggressiveness in three ways: through displacement of his affection to substitute figures representing "the incomparable father" (76); through his identification with God the Son and, after his father's death, with God the Father (76); through identification with William Gladstone, the English statesman who represented an earlier father image (85). In this way the authors explain Wilson's vendetta against Dean Andrew F. West of Princeton, whose efforts to establish a graduate college Wilson opposed unsuccessfully:

He seems to have taken in his unconscious the final step of full identification of himself with God only after his defeat at Princeton by West. Then, when his father was dead, and he was defeated by a father representative, he assumed his father's throne, became God in his unconscious and began to act with a sense of his own inevitable righteousness. (78)

This motive is iterated, without development or psychological embroidering, in a manner uncharacteristic of Freud. Wilson's breakdown in the spring of 1896 is accounted for in approximately the same way. For the previous seven years Wilson had been in relatively good health, he was happy, and his work had proved successful. What could explain his sudden low spirits and illness?

We shall probably be not far from the truth if we answer that the presence of his father in his home had excited his repressed aggressive activity against his father, and that this portion of his libido was without adequate outlet. (104)

The major evidence adduced for this aggressiveness is that of argumentative analogy: Wilson was *bound* to feel aggressive because adolescents normally do (74). Details are fitted to this explanation in the deductive manner indicated earlier: Wilson needed to compensate for a passive attitude toward his father —and was able to do so through identification with his mother's physical weakness and her "severity, shyness and aloofness"(66). This identification provides the main explanation for Wilson's failure to oppose Lloyd George and Clemenceau in negotiations after the war. He refused to employ the "masculine weapons" which his economic and political power had put into his hands, and insisted instead on using feminine persuasion:

> But to use those weapons involved a fight of precisely the sort he had never made and could not make in person, unless compelled to by his reaction-formation against his passivity to his father. He had never dared to have a fist fight in his life. All his fighting had been done with his mouth. (209)

If facts are misstated or glaring contradictions stand out, it is easy for the critic to say what is wrong, though the psychological insights may be powerful and substantial, as in the study of Leonardo. But in the absence of such misstatements and contradictions, the analysis is difficult to evaluate—except, as I have indicated, to point out that the very coherence of the argument is an indication of its weakness or failure. For everything has been explained in reductive fashion. An indirect and stronger test is to ask what general conclusions such a study is able to generate. The study of Woodrow Wilson does not meet this test well. The analyses of literary works do meet it and sometimes with extraordinary results.

V   *The Analysis of Literary Works*

Methods associated with dream interpretation are perhaps most prominent in studies of popular literature, particularly those in which patterns of imagery cannot be traced to mental conflict in individual writers. In these studies, Freud's concern is with general, widely established symbols such as he identifies in a 1911 essay on folklore: gold as a symbol of excrement, the Devil as "nothing else than the personification of the repressed unconscious instinctual life" (XII, 188). "Character and Anal Erotism"

(1908) shows how linguistic analysis derived from dream interpretation could be used to establish such meanings. Freud states that the identification of gold with excrement is supported by the original meanings of common words like "Mammon," a name for the Babylonian god of the underworld: "Thus, in following the usage of language, neurosis, here as elsewhere, is taking words in their original, significant sense, and where it appears to be using a word figuratively it is usually simply restoring its old meaning" (IX, 174).

These insights were extended in a short monograph of 1923, in which Freud analyzes the possessed states of the seventeenth-century painter Christoph Haizmann as a "demonological neurosis." The account of these possessions occurs in a contemporary scribal report and a personal statement by the painter himself. Haizmann, according to the account, claimed to have signed in blood a pact with the Devil, presumably to free himself of despondency. An exorcism led to recovery of the pact, but Haizmann continued to be tormented, this time by Jesus and the Virgin. He revealed now that there had been an even earlier pact, written in ink. The Devil had come to Haizmann at the time of his father's death and promised to relieve his despondency. Freud interpreted the pacts (which omitted the promise) as a means of replacing the lost father and so regaining the capacity to work, at the same time (in complex ways) expressing rebellion against a feminine attitude toward him. Freud generalizes from this evidence that God and the Devil were originally one figure, the split resulting from the characteristic ambivalence felt by human beings toward their fathers. Freud surmises that belief in the Devil as a condition for a strong belief in God (as in medieval Christianity) is explained not only by this split but by the "primal father," a "being of unlimited evil" (XIX, 86–87).

What keeps the studies in folklore and related topics from becoming handbook discourses is Freud's powerful generalizing and the insight he was able to provide into reader psychology. For example, the 1911 paper concludes by showing how the often indecent dreams of folklore could best be understood through the dream theory of psychoanalysis. They do much more than satisfy the "coarsest desires" of those they entertain: "It seems rather that behind these ugly façades are concealed mental reactions to impressions of life which are to be taken seriously, which even strike a sad note—reactions to which common people are ready to surrender, but only if they are accompanied by a yield of coarse pleasure" (XII, 203).

Various methods of analysis are joined in an instructive way in the remarkable 1913 essay, "The Theme of Three Caskets," concerned mainly with *The Merchant of Venice* and *King Lear*. Passing over differences in genre, language, and the dramatic uses of character, Freud seeks general patterns that will connect the plays with ancient folklore and fairy tales. Thus the three caskets that Bassanio must choose between are symbolic of women, and Freud knows this because in mythical and dramatic analogues a man chooses between three women. There is also the evidence of dreams: Freud would have so interpreted them if the play were a dream. The assumption that governs the analysis, in other words, is that the surface representation is invariably the product of secondary revision which censors forbidden meanings. And once he has shown that Bassanio is choosing between three women, Freud is able to develop the parallel with Lear who also must choose between three women.

The problem immediately arising is why Lear disowns Cordelia, who remains silent when she is asked to declare her love. Lear should recognize the "unassuming, speechless love" of his third daughter, but he does not (XII, 293). Freud depends on an ingenious deduction to solve this problem. Noting that analogues of the third (lead) casket—a third sister or a goddess—are conspicuously pale or silent, and that in dream and myth dumbness symbolizes death, he concludes that the third woman is the Goddess of Death—Atropos the inexorable. By extension the three sisters are then the Fates or Moirai of the ancient Greeks.

There is, however, an apparent contradiction; for these same third figures are young and beautiful and, like Portia and Cordelia, may be loving and life-giving. Freud's explanation is that contraries are often symbolized by a single figure in the unconscious; replacement and reaction formation are also operative, "and it is precisely in the revelation of such hidden forces as these that we look for the reward of this enquiry" (XII, 299). Thus, rebelling against the insight contained in the Moirai that death is a part of life, ancient man changed the Goddess of Death into the Goddess of Love. Indeed the mother goddesses of the ancient world were simultaneously creators of life and its de-

stroyers. The choice of Bassanio is consequently no choice whatever but a compulsion and must fall on the third of the caskets,
and he must do so "if every kind of evil is not to come about"
(XII, 300). And Freud extends these meanings even further.
Shakespeare has represented in *Lear*

the three inevitable relations that a man has with a woman—the woman
who bears him, the woman who is his mate and the woman who destroys
him; or that they are the three forms taken by the figure of the mother
in the course of a man's life—the mother herself, the beloved one who is
chosen after her pattern, and lastly the Mother Earth who receives him
once more. But it is in vain that an old man yearns for the love of
woman as he had it first from his mother; the third of the Fates alone,
the silent Goddess of Death, will take him into her arms. (XII, 301)

The passage does not reveal whether Freud understood that
Lear's other daughters in no way represent "the mother herself"
and "the beloved one who is chosen after her pattern." Goneril
and Regan are the very opposite of such conceptions. Such disparities are presumably irrelevant to our experience and interpretation of the play.

The reason is evident in the rhetorical structure that Freud has
been analyzing with such care. The power of the work of art derives not from the surface representation of character but from
the underlying pattern (three caskets, three women, three goddesses). The reader or viewer makes his response at the unconscious level:

We get an impression that a reduction of the theme to the original myth
is being carried out . . . so that we once more have a sense of the moving significance which had been weakened by the distortion. It is by
means of this reduction of the distortion, this partial return to the original, that the dramatist achieves his more profound effect upon us. (XII,
300)

Consistent with this view of literary experience, Freud extends
his rhetorical theory in the later essay on the uncanny, in the
statement that the emotional effect of certain works may be independent of the subject and content (XVII, 252).

Later formulations are consistent in stressing the greater importance of "latent" meanings in literary experience. Art, Freud
states in a 1913 paper on the applications of psychoanalysis, "con-

stitutes a region halfway between a reality which frustrates wishes and the wish-fulfilling world of the imagination—a region in which, as it were, primitive man's strivings for omnipotence are still in full force" (XIII, 188). We have seen that he was unwilling to attribute extraordinary or preternatural insight to the artist; and he in effect erased the mythology of a creative genius like Leonardo by showing that the capacity for sublimation could (and did) become undone. These attitudes are commensurate with his view, in the *Introductory Lectures*, that the artist is "in rudiments an introvert, not far removed from neurosis" (XVI, 376). It is the danger of neurosis, the often "partial inhibition of their efficiency," that Freud prefers to stress, and not the advantages of sublimation and the capacity for it that distinguishes artists from other people.

His analysis of Michelangelo's Moses (1914) illustrates one final use of dream interpretation in the appreciation of art. As in the analysis of *Gradiva*, all details of the work are important (the disparities of surface details and latent meanings too). Though he tended to stress major features that serve to disguise unconscious motives, no detail is assumed to be without significance. Thus the puzzling placement, in the statue, of the right index finger on the opposite strands of the beard finds its meaning in an imaginative reconstruction of the scene as the sculptor must have had it in mind—a reconstruction that gives attention to the least of the details. The seated Moses is suddenly startled by the worship of the Golden Calf:

He was sitting there calmly, we will suppose, his head with its flowing beard facing forward, and his hand in all probability not near it at all. Suddenly the clamor strikes his ear; he turns his head and eyes in the direction from which the disturbance comes, sees the scene and takes it in. Now wrath and indignation lay hold of him; and he would fain leap up and punish the wrongdoers, annihilate them. His rage, distant as yet from its object, is meanwhile directed in a gesture against his own body. His impatient hand, ready to act, clutches at his beard which has moved with the turn of his head, and presses it between his thumb and palm in the iron grasp of his closing fingers. . . . (XIII, 224–25)

The interpretation is complete only when each detail has been accounted for.

New insight leads Freud to revise this interpretation: Moses has been holding the tablets with his right hand. Losing hold of them at sight of the worshippers, he first thrusts his hand into his beard as though to turn his anger against himself, then withdraws his hand to keep the tablet from falling. Freud concludes that Michelangelo altered the Biblical account from "inner motives" and presented Moses as restraining his wrath—"of struggling successfully against an inward passion for the sake of a cause to which he has devoted himself "—both as a reproach to Julius II and as a criticism of himself (XIII, 233–34). Jones suggests that Freud was thinking of his own possible response to the defection of Adler and Jung. There is special significance, then, in the effort to keep the tablets from falling. As we suggested earlier, the artist, in this instance Freud as the imaginative critic of Michelangelo's sculpture, is by extension the spectator of his own work; and what he finds—what he is moved by sufficiently to impel a comment on it—must find a response in his own nature and experience. We are moved by works of art when impulses we have repressed are aroused or disturbed—and are maintained in a state of indeterminate feeling.

VI *"Some Character Types Met with in Psychoanalytic Work"*

Why indeterminacy should be important is indirectly answered in this highly influential essay of 1916, concerned ostensibly with unusual traits of patients, but chiefly devoted to characters of Shakespeare and Ibsen. The first two sections concern people who feel "exceptional" and people "wrecked by success"; the third concerns people who commit crimes to alleviate anxiety. The analysis of those "wrecked by success" provides part of the answer: the real fulfillment of repressed wishes triggers an "internal frustration." Ordinarily such frustration is triggered by a frustrating experience. In those "wrecked by success" the ego is using illness to defend itself against a wish tolerated so long as it remains in phantasy (XIV, 317). The ego, in other words, finds itself suspended—in an indeterminate state—in unexpected circumstances: the identical situation of the reader or viewer, though Freud does not say so. The other part of the answer is what I should like to term the rhetoric of concealment.

A main current of literary criticism in this century has been the formulation of a rhetoric that discloses fully the motives by which characters act and the norms by which they are to be judged. Critics who differ in their conceptions of form in art agree at least that form discloses, makes relationships luminous and brilliant, controls meaning by making it perceptible. The New Criticism, following the lead of Coleridge, based its definition of great literature on this premise, thus Tate's statement that "good poetry is a unity of all the meanings from the furthest extremes of intension and extension," that is, of ideas and experiences, all conscious and unconscious associations fully specified and organized.[5] Wimsatt says the same thing: "Every real poem is a complex poem, and only in virtue of its complexity does it have artistic unity."[6]

The implication of these statements is that, in unifying its disparate elements, the work of art makes even unconscious motives available to perception; for literary experience is what can be apprehended and enjoyed in a state of heightened awareness. A correlative idea is that the "truth" embodied in the work is a "public" truth" and can be judged by long-established standards. Private meanings of course exist but are irrelevant to our experience of the work and to its interpretation. For these critics "complexity of form is sophistication of content."[7] In short, the emotional power of a work is increased by the worth of the ideas we perceive or experience in it. The greater the mastery and transformation of emotion into thought, the greater the work. In the words of T. S. Eliot:

The poet who "thinks" is merely the poet who can express the emotional equivalent of thought. . . . To express precise emotion requires as great intellectual power as to express precise thought.[8]

This is not Freud's assumption; the dramatic power of a play like *Macbeth* does not depend on its intellectual cohesion or verisimilitude. For example, events may be crowded into a short period of time contrary to our sense of how things happen, but the emotional effect will be undisturbed; for "the economy of time in the tragedy expressly precludes a development of character from any motives but those inherent in the action itself" (XIV, 322). In other words, "action" is defined not simply by the surface events and relationships but by underlying patterns that we intuit. The murders of Duncan, Banquo, and Macduff's wife and children remain incredible until we understand that Macbeth is motivated not by mere ambition for himself but by torment over his childlessness: "It is not expressly stated in Holinshed that it was his childlessness which urged him to these courses, but enough time and room is given for that plausible motive" (XIV, 322). And, indeed, the dramatist may split a single character into complementary characters like Macbeth and his lady and preserve them as an imaginative unity. The power of the representation does not, then, depend on the cooperation of our intellectual powers but rather on the concealment of the springs of action. Concerning Ibsen's Rebecca West (in *Rosmersholm*) who suffers guilt arising from various wishes and acts, Freud states:

It is in fact a case of multiple motivation, in which a deeper motive comes into view behind the more superficial one. Laws of poetic economy necessitate this way of presenting the situation, for this deeper motive could not be explicitly enunciated. It had to remain concealed, kept from the easy perception of the spectator or the reader; otherwise serious resistances, based on the most distressing emotions, would have arisen, which might have imperilled the effect of the drama. (XIV, 329)

Freud drives home his point in noting, in the opening soliloquy of Shakespeare's *Richard the Third*, "a subtle economy of art in the poet that he does not permit his hero to give open and complete expression to all his secret motives" (XIV, 315). To disclose those motives fully would be to remove a necessary condition of powerful emotional experience. Howard Nemerov states this condition in suggesting that in poetry, "What is revealed . . . plays at being revealed."[9] In the Freudian formulation, ideas corresponding to the manifest content may be a disguise or facade for the latent content seeking expression through the deceptive "play" of surface meanings. This does not mean, however, that we are wholly denied understanding; but what understanding we do achieve comes after the experience itself:

The dramatist can indeed, during the representation, overwhelm us by his art and paralyze our powers of reflection; but he cannot prevent us from attempting subsequently to grasp its effect by studying its psychological mechanism. (XIV, 323)

A host of commentators have either repudiated or sought to reconcile Freud's essentially introvertive conception of art with a conception "in the service of life-in-culture," to quote Lionel Tril-

ling, or one reflective of the "integrative functions of the ego," in
the phrase of Ernst Kris.[10] Norman Holland, who emphasizes the
transformations of nuclear fantasy "toward social, moral, or intellectual meaning," suggests that art brings the full powers of man
into play:

> The aesthetic stance inhibits our motor activity; it therefore engages our
> moral and intellectual selves, not in suppressing or judging our deeper
> selves, but in accepting and transforming them. Our "rind" of higher
> ego-functions, our "core" of deeply regressed ego—these make up a
> richer, longer kind of self than our ordinary one.[11]

The thrust of Freud's thinking, I have been suggesting, was in
the opposite direction: toward concealment and even the decep-
tion of the intellectual powers as a way of heightening emotional
effect. Indeed the intellectual or moral character of an author
may be sorely deficient, as Dostoevsky shows. For the author of
The Brothers Karamazov—"the most magnificent novel ever written" (XXI, 177)—was a deceived moralist who identified himself
with the jailers of humanity (the Russian Czar and Church). He
was also a severe neurotic who was saved from becoming a crimi-
nal only by his turning inward his insatiable egoism and powerful
urge to destruction. The surface "truths" of his writings—the les-
sons he presumed to impart—in no way detract from his
achievement, however. What matters only is his powerful intuition and rendering of underlying psychological motives that join
writer and reader in concealed ways.

For the rhetoric of concealment has a dual purpose: to protect
both writer and reader from threatening motives arising in the
work, from "the most distressing emotions." The "creative artist"
in all of us must defend against the neurotic. To the extent that
art is an eruption of unconscious life, a compulsive activity, phantasy reshaped into "manifest" content—"poetic treatment is impossible without softening and disguise" (XXI, 188).

CHAPTER 6

Later Theoretical Writings

I Beyond the Pleasure Principle

WHEN the history of Freudian criticism is written, it will probably show in a majority of critics a dependence on the theory of sublimation, on the "rational" or moralizing operations of the secondary process, and in general on various formulas referring to the "pleasure principle." Even those who have leaned heavily on Freud's successors and stressed the integrative functions of art (ego-directed and therefore rational and constructive) have fitted their theories to one or more of these ideas instead of those stressing the regressive and introvertive qualities of art. Freud's own theory, by contrast, increasingly stressed the neurotic determinants and the compulsiveness in human behavior that is a major theme of his later theoretical writings.

This concern with the compulsions of our nature—not merely the sexual (which Freud had not earlier conceived in so dark a light) but the aggressive and destructive—had important consequences for his style of thought and writing. For the frame of discourse was broader and better suited to the deductive mode of argument perfected in the essays on metapsychology. Joined to this deductive mode was the dialectical: terms could be used with considerable freedom and extended at several levels, in the manner of Mill's *Three Essays on Religion*, in particular the famous essay on nature from which Freud could have learned how to synthesize definitions from traditional and current meanings. "Veracity might seem, of all virtues, to have the most plausible claim to being natural," Mill states, "since in the absence of motives to the contrary, speech usually conforms to, or at least does

not intentionally deviate from, fact." It is one of the purposes of
Freud's later writings to expose such deviations and their
motive—a purpose for which the later style is highly appropriate.

These points of style are seen in the important monograph of
1920, which introduced Freud's boldest and most controversial
instinctual theory—that of the Life and Death Instincts. The redefinition of earlier concepts is achieved now in a style in which
metaphor is the heart of exposition and no longer simply its mus-
cle. Consciousness is the "crust" of an originally undifferentiated
living substance or "vesicle," a "shield" or "membrane" that
forms to resist excitations from "an external world charged with
the most powerful energies." Once "baked through," it becomes
"to some degree inorganic," and excitations pass to the "next underlying layers, which have remained living, with only a fragment
of their original intensity." Through its "death" this crust or
"outer layer has saved all the deeper ones from a similar
fate"—unless excitations manage to break through it (XVIII,
26–27).

In general, the problem of style is to portray the forces of mind
without making a mystery of them, while at the same time relating them to traditional metaphysical concepts that gain precision
in the context of psychoanalysis. In fact, psychoanalysis is ready
now, Freud indicates, to explain the Kantian proposition that
space and time are "necessary forms of thought." Whereas unconscious processes are timeless, the idea of time derives from consciousness and perception: "This mode of functioning may
perhaps constitute another way of providing a shield against
stimuli" (XVIII, 28). The exchange of terms, different levels of
generality, and the indeterminate metaphor make possible the extension of ideas in such a way that psychological and biological
reality are joined to the philosophical without a delimiting of
boundary. The formulation of consciousness already quoted implies that the energies forming the unconscious and impinging
upon the organism are biological in origin; but there is the implication too of a purposiveness or aim that is vitalistic rather than
material: the word "living" is both general and specific, literal
and metaphoric. This style of exposition is perhaps best illustrated by a reference to Plato's *Symposium* in support of the view
that at least one instinct in man may be conservative, seeking to
restore an earlier untroubled existence:

Shall we follow the hint given us by the poet-philosopher [Aristophanes in his fable of the original androgyne], and venture upon the hypothesis that living substance at the time of its coming to life was torn apart into small particles, which have ever since endeavored to reunite through the sexual instincts? (XVIII, 58)

The Death Instinct itself is represented through this kind of exposition. Freud arrived at the concept through two experiences that affected him greatly—observation of his grandson at play and observation of traumatized soldiers. In both instances there was an evident compulsion to repeat which could not be explained by the original postulate of self-preservative and sexual instincts or its revision in the essays on narcissism and on metapsychology. His new formulation avoided the conclusion (implied in the 1914 essay) that all instinctual life is libidinal (comprising ego and object instincts) and thus negating the dualism on which conflict is predicated. Freud distinguished now between the Life Instinct (Eros)—comprising the ego and object instincts deriving from narcissistic libido—and the Death Instinct, an inherent "urge" to restore an earlier existence, a basic "inertia" in organic life (XVIII, 36). The "pleasure principle," seeking to reduce excitations or bring them to zero, serves the Death Instinct, conceived as "beyond" or prior to it: Eros itself, as Plato and others had intuited, seeks to reunite the "splintered fragments of living substance" (XVIII, 58). The traumatic neuroses could now be explained: traumatic dreams are retrospective preparations for anxiety, serving to allay the stimuli that cause trauma and clear the way for "pleasure."

Ricoeur points out that Freud did not (as he seems to have thought) reject older distinctions and oppositions:

We need only consider that the new dualism is located not on the level of purposes, aims, and objects, but on the level of *forces*; hence we must not try to make the duality of ego-instincts and sexual instincts coincide with the duality of life instincts and death instincts. The latter dualism cuts across *each* of the forms of the libido. . . . Object-love is both life instinct *and* death instinct; narcissistic love is Eros unaware of itself *and* clandestine cultivation of death. Sexuality is at work wherever death is at work.[1]

This conservation of ideas derives surely from the impulse to generalize without discarding observations that Freud felt were pioneering. Other definitions and formulations illustrate this conservative tendency. Thus "artistic play and artistic imitation carried out by adults . . . do not spare the spectators (for instance, in tragedy) the most painful experiences and can yet be felt by them as highly enjoyable" (XVIII, 17). The compulsive dimension of artistic, indeed of all, activity is now the central consideration: what seems to be "an untiring impulsion towards further perfection"—an "instinct towards perfection"—is not willed or freely chosen but a compulsion resulting from "instinctual repression upon which is based all that is most precious in human civilization." Since the "backward path" is blocked by the resistances that maintain repression, "there is no alternative but to advance in the direction in which growth is still free—though with no prospect of bringing the process to a conclusion or of being able to reach the goal" (XVIII, 42).

II *"The Economic Problem in Masochism"*

The powerful and encompassing insights attained are generated as much by the style of reasoning as by the theory itself. The short, highly condensed 1924 essay on masochism shows this clearly, and for this reason its main ideas are worth considering in detail. Essentially the process of generalization is accomplished through an extension of terms that conserves earlier definitions and theories. Freud's basic argument is that Eros and the Death Instinct have escaped notice for so long because in the course of human development they intermingle and fuse. "Moral masochism"—as distinguished from erotogenic and feminine masochism—is the "classical piece of evidence" for instinctual fusion (XIX, 170).

The chief terms redefined and extended in the essay are "sadism" and "masochism." Freud indicates that aggressive impulses are manifestations of the Death Instinct. In the course of development, libido succeeds in turning this instinct away from the individual and toward the world through the agency of the muscular and skeletal systems; the instinct is "then called the destructive instinct, the instinct for mastery, or the will to power" (XIX, 163). A portion of the instinct also serves the sexual function as a "true sadism," by means of which the loved object is momentarily overpowered, and that portion which is "operative" in the body—"primal sadism"—is roughly equivalent or identical to masochism (XIX, 164). Once a certain portion of this masochism has been also diverted away from the individual, the remainder acts as "erotogenic masochism" and merges with the sexual libido, taking the self for its object.

On what seems to be an analogy with other processes, Freud speculates on the existence of a secondary masochism:

We shall not be surprised to hear that in certain circumstances the sadism, or instinct of destruction, which has been directed outwards, projected, can be once more introjected, turned inwards, and in this way regress to its earlier situation. If this happens, a secondary masochism is produced, which is added to the original masochism. (XIX, 164)

Analogy also guides the statement that erotogenic masochism passes through the developmental stages of the sexual libido: the anal-sadistic, phallic, and genital stages generate the "changing psychical coatings" or phantasies associated with feminine masochism in men, including beating by the father, castration, coitus, and childbirth. The particular psychological disposition or sexual character of the feminine masochist depends on the developmental stage at which fixation occurs; that is, he may be impotent and derive sexual gratification solely from his phantasies, or, as Freud indicates in his 1919 essay on beating phantasies, he may unite his masochism with genital activity to carry out normal intercourse (aided by masochistic phantasies).

Both the feminine and the moral masochist suffer from guilt. The difference is that the moral masochist endures suffering for its own sake; the condition that it be inflicted by the loved one is of no importance. "It may even be caused by impersonal powers or by circumstances; the true masochist always turns his cheek whenever he has a chance of receiving a blow" (XIX, 165). The connection with sexual motives thus appears to be severed. The moral masochist is, however, different from the ultra-moralist for whom the sadism of the superego is the source of guilt. In the moral masochist, the source of guilt is masochism in the ego seeking punishment from the superego (that is, from internalized parental imagos) or from actual parental figures.

From this highly technical distinction Freud now derives a series of generalizations which considerably enlarge his frame of reference. Whereas the ultra-moralist experiences the sadism of the superego consciously, the moral masochist remains unaware of the masochism of the ego (or at least these are the usual situations). As a result of this unconsciousness, the moral masochist's ethical sense may be exceedingly strong—unless much of his conscience disappears into his masochism and he is tempted to commit sinful acts to provoke the sadistic conscience.[2] He may also seek to destroy his chances of success in the world by persuading himself that he is fated to unhappiness and bad luck. So powerful is moral masochism that the explanation previously offered is insufficient; only a strong libidinal element can explain that power and must be reintroduced. The unconscious sense of guilt, or (more correctly) the "need for punishment," is really a need for punishment from the parental figure a "regressive distortion" of the wish to have sexual relations with the father:

If we insert this explanation into the content of moral masochism, its hidden meaning becomes clear to us. Conscience and morality have arisen through the overcoming, the desexualization, of the Oedipus complex; but through moral masochism morality becomes sexualized once more, the Oedipus complex is revived and the way is opened for a regression from morality to the Oedipus complex. (XIX, 169)

The enlargement of ideas traced here—their extension through a genetic account of two primal forces—is qualified only in the correction of an earlier view. The "Nirvana principle"—the "tendency to stability" associated with the Death Instinct in *Beyond the Pleasure Principle*—is not after all identical with the pleasure principle but was transformed by Eros into the pleasure principle to serve its needs.

III   The Ego and the Id

The second major alteration in psychoanalytic theory came with the division of consciousness and the unconscious into the ego, superego, and id. I do not presume here to give a full account of Freud's ideas and complex thinking on a range of problems connected with the structural hypothesis. I shall limit myself to suggesting how the theoretical problem was shaped by the semantic—how semantic distinctions were able to shape the selection and interpretation of evidence.

To review the situation briefly, Freud found it necessary to reformulate the unconscious because he had been using the term both to characterize a mental state and to denote a structure of the mind. In the latter sense what had been repressed in experience was "unconscious," in Freud's words, "which is not, in itself and without more ado, capable of becoming conscious" (XIX, 15). In other words, there had to be a place where repressions survived. Having postulated the ego and loosely associated it with consciousness, he was forced to recognize their inequivalence, for the ego plainly resisted certain truths or insights, and such resistance indicates that the ego must have an unconscious side or layer.

Freud solved the problem by retaining the term "unconscious" as a description of mental experience and substituting the id as the "reservoir" of libido, the primary reality whose modification by the external world is the ego. Topographically he conceived ego as "an extension of the surface differentiation" (XIX, 25), the apparatus which controls motility. In *The Question of Lay Analysis* Freud warned that reference to spatial relations is merely to "the regular succession of functions," and he adds a few paragraphs later:

In psychology we can only describe things by the help of analogies. There is nothing peculiar in this; it is the case elsewhere as well. But we have constantly to keep changing these analogies, for none of them lasts us long enough. (XX, 194–95)

We have seen, however, that he was prone to ignore this qualification and treat analogy as fact in exposition. Though he refers to the "value of a 'fiction' " in establishing scientific hypotheses (XX, 194), he was no longer thinking with heuristic concepts. Once conceived, Eros and Thanatos, for example, were henceforth eternal forces in conflict. Their manifestation in individual human life indicates that tragic human nature is grounded in the nature of existence itself.

Another way of expressing the difference between ego and id is through the concept of identification—perhaps a mode of conservation of energy in nature itself, though Freud does not state this. The id gives up objects it has cathected only when these are instituted in the ego, defined as "a precipitate of abandoned object-cathexes" (XIX, 29). In this precipitate lies the origin of the superego, another name for the "ego-ideal" postulated in the theory of narcissism. In other words, the superego is an outcome of the Oedipus complex, "a residue of the earliest object-choices of the id" (XIX, 34)—of parental imagos introjected and serving as a policeman of the ego, following the surrender of the parents as love objects. Freud did not propose to locate the superego topographically, or "to work it into any of the analogies with the help of which we have tried to picture the relation between the ego and the id" (XIX, 36–37).

As in *Beyond the Pleasure Principle*, Freud sought to simplify and also conserve the formulations of twenty-five years or more. Thus the id was identified not only with the erotic and death instincts but with the pleasure principle, and the ego with perception and the reality principle:

Moreover, the ego seeks to bring the influence of the external world to bear upon the id and its tendencies, and endeavors to substitute the reality principle for the pleasure principle which reigns unrestrictedly in the id. For the ego, perception plays the part which in the id falls to instinct. The ego represents what may be called reason and common sense, in contrast to the id, which contains the passions. (XIX, 25)

Perhaps aware that he had loosened these terms to generalize broadly, Freud qualifies the statement as "holding good on the average or 'ideally.' " But more important, such normative statements made it possible to project an average human character, not implied in a purely developmental psychology, but necessary to statements about man in his cultural setting.

So strongly embedded in his thinking seems to have been the assumption of conflicting mental agencies that Freud could not avoid representing them as separate entities even though, theoretically, the ego is "merely a specially differentiated part" of the id (XX, 97). The writings of this period in general tend to be ambiguous on the question of the relative strength of the ego in dealing with the id. Thus Freud states in *Inhibitions, Symptoms and Anxiety*:

Although the act of repression demonstrates the strength of the ego, in one particular it reveals the ego's powerlessness and how impervious to influence are the separate instinctual impulses of the id. For the mental process which has been turned into a symptom owing to repression now maintains its existence outside the organization of the ego and independently of it. (XX, 97)

Freud goes on to discuss the integrative and defensive powers of the ego, but later comments on the difficulty of dealing with repression call into question its stability and health (XX, 153). There seems, in fact, to be no stage at which the ego is free from danger. Symptom formation would seem to be a nearly continuous process, providing important gains, though Freud is at pains to deny that the ego "heals" easily around the "foreign body" represented by the symptoms. It has created a symptom mainly to enjoy its advantages, he points out (XX, 99).

Such theoretical considerations were, of course, taken to be consistent with clinical evidence, and Freud does return to earlier cases for corroboration or review, but in the main his concern is with consistency in his definitions. His examination of the question of whether anxiety is a response of the id or of the ego is but one example (XX, 140). This style of thought is to be found in *The Question of Lay Analysis*, written in a popular style mainly as a dialogue between a doctor and an "Impartial Person." Here the ambiguity in the characterization is even more pronounced, perhaps because of the idea that "a part of the id remains forbidden ground to the ego" (XX, 203). Theoretically this ought not to be so, for "there is no natural opposition between ego and id; they belong together, and under healthy conditions cannot in practice be distinguished from each other" (XX, 201). Yet the ego seems to lose the influence it exerted before it embarked on repression and seems prone to neurotic disorder; at least the weight of this consideration in the whole discussion implies this much. In general, the ego seems relatively feeble, measured by the energy-laden id.

The statement in *Beyond the Pleasure Principle* that the ego represents reason and common sense—the conception of the "rational" ego in *The Ego and the Id*—is unrepresentative of Freud's actual view. The unconscious portion of the ego, in which are seated powerful resistances to new perceptions that would undo repression and neurotic symptoms, is shown by clinical experience to be a powerful determinant of mental life, more powerful than the conscious portion. The force of the unconscious superego, which also opposes the patient's recovery through its fostering of guilt and the desire for punishment, intensifies this power. The implication throughout these writings is that a mental force is powerful by virtue of being unconscious, not by virtue of its origin in the id, even though the id provides the energies of the ego and superego. Indeed Freud states in the *New Introductory Lectures* that, "in its blind efforts for the satisfaction of its instincts," the id depends on the ego to escape destruction (XXII, 75). In short, the unconsciousness of motives is the real source of their power and not the energies of the id which remain constant and invariable.

For these energies are indestructible and therefore present in the mind from the beginning. They are not generated by or from experience as unconscious motives of experience may be. This assumption in Freud's thinking was undoubtedly strengthened by his reading of Schopenhauer, for whom the "will" is indestructible though capable of renouncing pleasure.[3] In a passage which the editors of the *Standard Edition* believe strongly influenced Freud, Schopenhauer identifies the will with "sexual passion" (*Geschlechtstrieb*), and indeed with "the effort to sustain the species" which "must be more powerful in proportion as the life of the species surpasses that of the individual in duration, extension and value" (XIX, 224). It is the assumption that he was dealing with an indestructible energy—not with its agency or seat in the mind—that probably accounts for the emphasis in so many passages on the impulsive qualities of experience, even though there is a basis in Freud's later instinctual theory for a contrary emphasis. The popular and somewhat inaccurate idea of the id as seething with libido probably derives from this emphasis, as well as from references to its "locomotive energy" and similar metaphorical descriptions (XXII, 77).

Whatever inconsistencies resulted from so deductive and rhetorical an analysis, there were compensations in its power to generate new questions and insights. Freud now was dealing with problems that had eluded satisfactory answers. The harshness of conscience was one of these: Freud now was able to show that identifications that form the superego are "in the nature of a desexualization or even of a sublimation"—the result being an instinctual defusion that releases the destructive instincts. These account for the harshness of the superego. He was now also able to explain why "the more a man controls his aggressiveness, the more intense becomes his ideal's inclination to aggressiveness against his ego" (XIX, 54). The earlier theory of mind had not provided so profound an explanation.

These various formulations illustrate a mode of thought, a discourse which is explorative and therefore tentative and open to new possibilities of definition and experience. For the passions were for Freud, in Rieff's words, "autonomous and unexplained"; his imagination was Stoic. The need for an open discourse explains the open form of so many of the essays—on a wide range of topics from a childhood memory in Goethe's *Dichtung and Wahrheit* to experiences of transience and the "uncanny" and the termination of therapy. The open form permitted Freud to treat a large number of topics, often very loosely related, in a single extended discussion. "Dostoevsky and Parricide" is one notable example, with the interspersed discussions of Greek and Shakespearean tragedy and the psychoanalytic view of parricide, and with the turn at the end to a novel of Stefan Zweig.

I have avoided using the word "philosophical" to characterize Freud's achievement in the essay and in the longer writings because of the denigration it carries in some assessments that deny the importance of the later theoretical ideas; but it is fitting to use it now. I suggested earlier that Freud was the stylistic successor of Mill, whose essays are a revelation of the personal self—of man thinking. But most of all he resembles the stoical Montaigne in his openness of mind and his awareness that thought, like the essay itself, is a beginning always.[4]

IV *The Problem of Analysis*

The need for openness of mind and cultivation of awareness is nowhere better indicated than in Freud's discussion of "transference." In one of his papers on the technique of psychoanalysis, written in 1914, Freud summarized its role in bringing the patient's "compulsion to repeat" under control and substituting for it the process of remembering. The compulsion is made useful by permitting it to "assert itself in a definite field." In the "playground" of transference, it expresses itself without restriction, revealing as it does so everything pathogenic in the patient's mind. "The transference thus creates an intermediate region between illness and real life through which the transition from the one to the other is made" (XII, 154). Analysis is thus not so rational or orderly a cure as might be thought. The true source of cure, Freud indicates in *The Question of Lay Analysis*, is "the wish-fulfilling activity of the imagination." Nor is this activity always equal to dealing with the resistances encountered: "There are cases in which one cannot master the unleashed transference and the analysis has to be broken off; but one must at least have struggled with the evil spirits to the best of one's strength" (XX, 227). A brief comment in the 1940 *Outline* represents, perhaps, Freud's final view: "The ideal conduct for our purposes," he states, "would be that he [the patient] should behave as normally as possible outside the treatment and express his abnormal reactions only in the transference" (XXIII, 177).

The meaning of the resistances—of the "compulsion to repeat"—eluded Freud's understanding until the formulation of the Death Instinct illuminated the role of aggression in normal human behavior. That role could be understood only as a general force in all people, not simply in the sick and neurotic—just as anxiety could be understood only when examined as a normal, constant response of all people to traumatic experiences. Freud's intuition of this fact perhaps encouraged him to externalize the sources of conflict, of extending its field, in his final instinctual theory. Eros and Thanatos were eternal forces, not merely instinctual phenomena of indeterminate origin, and reason was helpless against them.[5]

Freud's tragic view was now centered in a conflict of instincts and external imperatives now fully declared. Psychoanalysis and philosophy were joined in the 1937 essay "Analysis Terminable and Interminable," perhaps his most definitive statement of this tragic view. Beginning with a consideration of proposals for shortening the period of analysis, Freud moves to factors that delay recovery, and shows these to be so powerful that analysis must finally be considered interminable. Since the "normal" ego is a "fiction," all that is possible is the securing of "the best possible psychological conditions for the functions of the ego" (XXIII, 239, 250). There are, in fact, certain psychological phenomena that can only be explained by the intrusion of a force that was late-coming. The incapacity of the heterosexual to tolerate homosexual feeling, for example, could not be explained by a limited "quota of libido" available for the struggle of conflicting impulses; and the conflict itself defies explanation. Why should the available libido not be divided and maintained in balance? Freud concludes:

the tendency to a conflict is something special, something which is newly added to the situation, irrespective of the quantity of libido. An independently-emerging tendency to conflict of this sort can scarcely be attributed to anything but the intervention of an element of free aggressiveness. (XXIII, 244)

The wording of the statement suggests that the instinct is taken to be a general imperative. Eros is not, in this context, coequal in its force, though in the discussion of Empedocles that follows love and strife are conceived as "everlastingly at war" (XX, 246). The analogy is not exact, for destructiveness finally has its way in the individual, with the cessation of conflict in death.

The thrust of the argument is that the analyst must not become persuaded that his own clear understanding is a measure of the patient's. There remains the intractable human unknown, inaccessible to analysis, which "in claiming to cure neuroses by ensuring control over instinct, is always right in theory but not always right in practice" (XXIII, 229).

This deceptively objective statement reveals Freud's divided state of mind and the tensions of his thought. The style of the whole essay is rational and severely objective, without the personal note of earlier monographs. Yet the long consideration of factors working against the termination of analysis builds the impression of the enormous and ultimately intractable complexity of mind. The charge that Freud's view of man is a reductive one will not stand in the face of these insights. If the normal ego is a fiction, so is the idea of the healthy ego. "Where id was, there ego shall be," Freud states in the *New Introductory Lectures*, but the difficulty is now seen to be immense: "It is a work of culture—not unlike the draining of the Zuider Zee" (XXII, 80).

Freud can merely restate the dilemma and impasse, and his impulse throughout the 1930's is a scientific reduction of his ideas, "in the most concise form and in the most unequivocal terms," he states in the preface to the *Outline*, "not to compel belief or to arouse conviction" (XXIII, 144). The style of the late writings may give the impression of an equanimity of mind; the content attests to Freud's deepening conviction that human nature is unalterably tragic.[6]

V *The Nature of Thinking*

There was one hope for man, nevertheless, and that was his capacity for scientific thought. The nature of the intellectual process had been a concern of Freud over a lifetime, and he brought his many ideas to completion in the *New Introductory Lectures*. In "Thoughts on War and Death" (1915) he had made the tentative suggestion that man's intellectual life begins with his ambivalent feelings over the death of persons loved and hated (XIV, 293). A related idea in the 1908 essay on the sexual theories of children is that their brooding and doubt is the model of later intellectual activity directed to problem-solving (IX, 219). And the 1925 essay on negation indicates that in therapy the content of repressed ideas becomes conscious only through negation itself. Freud's characteristic view seems to have been that the antithesis between subject and object arises through loss of something valuable: "But it is evident that a precondition for the setting up of reality-testing is that objects shall have been lost which once brought real satisfaction." The "polarity of judgment" itself —affirmation and negation—could be accounted for through the new instinctual theory, Eros promoting unity and the Death Instinct expulsion or negation. (XIX, 238–39)

Negation is, in fact, the source of whatever liberating power thought may possess. As psychotic thinking shows, the impulse to negation is probably "a sign of a defusion of instincts that has taken place through a withdrawal of the libidinal components." Judgment itself becomes possible only when "the creation of the symbol of negation has endowed thinking with a first measure of freedom from the consequences of repression and, with it, from the compulsion of the pleasure principle" (XIX, 239). Scientific inquiry—based on totally uninhibited thinking—might by implication show the way out of the human impasse, and it is perhaps with this idea in mind that Freud devotes a major portion of the *New Introductory Lectures* to the "best hope for the future . . . that intellect—the scientific spirit, reason—may in process of time establish a dictatorship in the mental life of man"

(XXII, 171). And Freud is careful to indicate that scientific thinking is only a special kind of ordinary thinking, its particular features being a disinterested curiosity, an avoidance of "individual factors and affective influences," a trust in sense perception and experimentation (XXII, 170).

In an earlier essay, "Psychoanalysis and Telepathy," Freud expressed the fear that the triumph of occultism would lead to the collapse of scientific investigation of unknown forces. The possibility of a supernatural reality offended his image of man in his ideal setting—a restless Promethean figure, struggling to master phantasy and discover an objective reality. The interest in the occult, he states in the *Lectures*, is perhaps a disguised effort to aid religion. The thrust of the concluding lecture on the *Weltanschauung* of psychoanalysis is that religion is not merely the rival of science but its enemy, and indeed the enemy of progress. If religion succeeds in bringing under control fear of demons and in institutionalizing ethical ideas without which man cannot exist, it nevertheless remains a form of wish fulfillment that bears the mark of infantile thought: "Its consolations deserve no trust. Experience teaches us that the world is no nursery" (XXII, 168). Psychoanalysis has no *Weltanschauung* of its own, Freud states, none except that of the scientific method itself:

If what we believe were really a matter of indifference, if there were no such thing as knowledge distinguished among our opinions by corresponding to reality, we might build bridges just as well out of cardboard as out of stone, we might inject our patients with a decagram of morphine instead of a centigram, and might use tear-gas as a narcotic instead of ether. But even the intellectual anarchists would violently repudiate such practical applications of their theory. (XXII, 176)

Freud rises in these pages to an eloquence unmatched in his other writings; the style is now frequently epigrammatic, in anticipation of the concision of the final *Outline*. The *New Introductory Lectures* speak for the scientist. But there remained his intense pessimism, reflected in a series of writings on anthropology, culture and religion, now to be considered.

CHAPTER 7

Neurosis and Culture

I Totem and Taboo

THOUGH Freud had commented on the origins of culture in earlier writings, *Totem and Taboo* (1913) was his first extended treatment of the topic. An important impetus to the work was his growing disillusionment with Jung, part of whose *Transformations and Symbols of the Libido* he read in manuscript. His reading of Frazer, whose *Totemism and Exogamy* he drew upon for many of his ideas, was another. Freud considered *Totem and Taboo,* particularly the fourth part dealing with the killing of the primal father, one of his finest. And indeed the work is the seminal one of his later years, generating the ideas that eventually constituted a thorough critique of modern civilization. His wish to generalize from these hypothetical ideas is evident in his statement in the preface that taboos express "in a negative form and directed towards another subject-matter" the psychological content of the Kantian categorical imperative: an idea he was fond of referring to in other works. Indeed the concern with imperatives that stand outside the subjective, psychological reality of the individual shapes the argument in important ways. The nature of that argument—building to a definition of the single important social imperative—is worth considering in detail.

The ideas on the nature of thinking just considered are presented in *Totem and Taboo* in somewhat different form. Freud's general premise is that the thinking of primitive man, and in particular animism and the system of taboos, arise from man's propensity to connect his experiences:

There is an intellectual function in us which demands unity, connection and intelligibility from any material, whether of perception or thought, that comes within its grasp; and if, as a result of special circumstances, it is unable to establish a true connection, it does not hesitate to fabricate a false one. (XIII, 95)

The model for this activity is the "secondary revision" of dream materials, and it is found too in phobias, obsessional thinking, and delusional disorders. Freud states the common features in an important passage:

Thus a system is best characterized by the fact that at least two reasons can be discovered for each of its products: a reason based upon the premises of the system (a reason, then, which may be delusional) and a concealed reason, which we must judge to be the truly operative and the real one. (XIII, 95–96)

A second and related premise is that living and thinking are achievements connected with the human disposition to neurosis; in Freud's words, "instinctual repression [is] a measure of the level of civilization that has been reached" (XIII, 97).

These premises stand behind an inductive argument from analogy between obsessional behavior and primitive customs, qualified by the warning that the analogy may be in "externals" only and not in "essential character," for "Nature delights in making use of the same forms in the most various biological connections" (XIII, 26). At the end of the work, he qualifies the analogy again: though neurotics and primitive man fail to distinguish between thinking and acting, primitive man is by contrast uninhibited: the deed substitutes for the thought. These qualifications are, however, little attended to, indeed are ignored later in the consideration of the origins of religion. That primitive man *is* neurotic is implied in the sexualized quality of his thinking: a component source of neurosis in modern man is the survival of this primitive disposition:

As regards neurotics, we find that on the one hand a considerable part of this primitive attitude has survived in their constitution, and on the other hand that the sexual repression that has occurred in them has brought about a further sexualization of their thinking processes. (XIII, 89)

The question that arises is what exactly is transmitted, if not inherited. If the memory of actual events is transmitted, the importance of impulse would be accordingly diminished—contrary to Freud's earlier discovery of their primacy in neurosis. Instead of dealing with the specific problems of a "collective mind," he indicates that social psychology is to be explained mainly through "the inheritance of psychical dispositions" and adds that "everyone possesses in his unconscious mental activity an apparatus which enables him to interpret other people's reactions, that is, to undo the distortions which other people have imposed on the expression of their feelings" (XIII, 158–59). All that can be said with any certainty is that "the mere hostile *impulse*" against the primal father, the "mere existence of a wishful *phantasy*" of his murder and devourment would have been a sufficient cause of the remorse that produced totemism and taboo (XIII, 159–60).

Like obsessional symptoms, taboos are without a clear motive; are grounded in a feeling of psychic necessity; are displaceable (which explains the fear that contact with a tabooed person or object will infect the community); and give rise to ceremonial observances. Taboos are grounded in two laws of totemism: the non-killing of the totem animal, and avoidance of sexual intercourse with those of the opposite sex in the totem clan. Drawing his examples chiefly from Frazer, Freud indicates that taboo and totemism exhibit opposing trends corresponding to the child's ambivalent attitude toward the father. Elevating the king is often motivated by hostility or spite, but there is also affection strong enough to explain remorse. Taboo observances have a double purpose: to enforce renunciation through mourning, and to disguise the unconscious hostility and conceal temptation:

The taboo upon the dead arises . . . from the contrast between conscious pain and unconscious satisfaction over the death that has occurred. . . . The fact that a dead man is helpless is bound to act as an encouragement to the survivor to give free rein to his hostile passions, and that temptation must be countered by a prohibition. (XIII, 61)

This distinction between conscious pain and unconscious pleasure explains why taboo ceremonials have the repetitive characteristic of obsessional acts and thus give rise to religious observance. The taboo simultaneously exalts the king and reduces him to a torment and slavery worse than any of his subjects endures. And here is the precise analogy to obsessional neurosis in which the repressed and the repressing impulse are satisfied simultaneously: "The obsessional act is *ostensibly* a protection against the prohibited act; but *actually*, in our view, it is a repetition of it" (XIII, 50). Freud also cites emotional ambivalence as the basis of conscience.

Freud proceeds through further analogies to an explanation of a number of primitive practices, for example, imitative and contagious magic. These exhibit an overvaluation of mental activity, the subordination of things to ideas about them. The connections established in thought are assumed to hold between objects in reality. Thought itself in this situation is sexualized, and in primitive man constitutes an "intellectual narcissism." By contrast, in modern man omnipotence has surrendered to the reality principle, the external world having become the object of desire, except in art which retains the magical properties of primitive thought. On the analogy with the libidinal development in human beings, beginning with the narcissistic stage and progressing to object choice and, finally, the establishing of the reality principle, Freud distinguishes three stages in the evolving view of the universe: the animistic, in which primitive man attributes omnipotence to his thoughts and consequently himself; the religious, in which omnipotence is transferred to the gods, though some is reserved to the human being; and the scientific, in which omnipotence is wholly surrendered.

The best-known and most important ideas in *Totem and Taboo* derived from W. Robertson Smith's *Religion of the Semites* (1889). Freud combined these speculations with those of Frazer and Darwin among others. The totem meal originated in the killing of the primal father by his sons who united to destroy the patriarchal horde, their motive being to erase his power and sexual dominance. But the primal father was envied, too, so that his devourment meant the acquisition of his strength—in other words, an identification with him. Owing to the affection that had been necessarily suppressed, guilt immediately set in, with the result that the dead man achieved a power in death he had not exerted in life. Accordingly, a totem animal was substituted, and prohibitions were established. The deed was revoked by outlawing the killing of the totem and resigning the women of the primal father. Incest taboos followed, for none of the brothers was strong enough to replace the father. Totemic religion—marked by a commemorative feast—expressed both remorse at the original act and victory over the father. As we have noted, the ambivalence originating in the father complex accounts for the repetitiveness of these ceremonials. Parricide occurred repeatedly in the killing and eating of the totem animal in sacrificial rites, in part as a way of retaining the attributes which new circumstances weakened or almost annihilated.

The ancient gods originated later, as the bitter memory of the primal father faded, and affection that had been present grew increasingly powerful. The new paternal deities represented the total power that the dead father possessed. With the alteration of the totem feast into new ceremonials, the totem animal became merely a sacrificial offering. The new arrangement made possible a greater alleviation of guilt, for the heirs of the original horde of sons no longer consciously demanded the sacrifice of themselves. The sacrifice is now required and regulated by God, and myths of this period show Him killing the totem animal, that is, Himself: the most extreme expression of denial of the primal crime. In a concluding comment Freud unites the internal, psychological reality with the external. The final conception of sacrifice

expresses satisfaction at the earlier father-surrogate having been abandoned in favor of the superior concept of God. At this point the psychoanalytic interpretation of the scene coincides approximately with the allegorical, surface translation of it, which represents the god as overcoming the animal side of his own nature. (XIII, 150)

The analogical argument that we have been tracing is completed in the analysis of Christianity and the brief discussion of Greek tragedy. The parallel between religion and obsessional neurosis had long been in Freud's mind. He had stated in the earlier "Obsessive Acts and Religious Practices" (1907) that obsessional neurosis "presents a travesty, half comic and half tragic, of a private religion" (IX, 119) and suggested that the "petty ceremonials" come to dominate as a way of shifting attention away from their motives. As he was to indicate in *Future of an Illusion* fourteen years later, Christianity (with other world religions) is the "universal neurosis," though why is not directly stated since the analogy is not intended to be exact. Briefly, Christianity offered a new alternative to the assuagement of guilt: the sacrifice of the "son" for the guilt inherited from the primal horde. Atonement was more complete than heretofore because the women of the primal father were now renounced totally. The "inexorable psychological law of ambivalence" came into play, however, for the deed of atonement fulfilled the hostility of the son toward the father; that is, through his own death the son became God. The ambivalence is felt most strongly by the worshippers, for in the ritual Communion which resurrects the ancient totem feast they seek "sanctity" in consuming the blood and flesh of the son. Yet because the son has become God Himself, they are actually participating in a "fresh elimination" of the primal father, "a repetition of the guilty deed" (XIII, 154–55). Christianity therefore, by implication, continues to reinforce the repressions that generate neurotic guilt.

Though Freud states that the sacrifice of the son was an undisguised admission of the original murder, the implication of the whole discussion, and in particular the consideration of psychological ambivalence, is that the meaning of these acts remains unconscious. The 1907 essay had made this point explicitly: "In all believers . . . the motives which impel them to religious practices are unknown to them or are represented in consciousness by others which are advanced in their place" (IX, 122–23). The brief succeeding discussion of Greek tragedy in *Totem and Taboo* also implies this unconscious factor, as the tragic hero represents the primal father and the Chorus the rebellious children whose guilt the hero redeems through his death. Both hero and chorus presumably enact ambivalent roles, the motives of their speeches and actions being never fully expressed, for the "scene upon the stage was derived from the historical scene through a process of systematic distortion—one might even say, as the product of a refined hypocrisy" (XIII, 156).

Whether in religion, obsessional neurosis, or art, powerful effects or attachments depend on unconscious, concealed meanings, on the shift of attention to "petty ceremonials" or to formal qualities whose appeal is diversionary.[1] The repetitiveness that characterizes ritual as well as dramatic action underscores this dependence, and though Freud does not draw such an inference in this discussion, so too does the primal repression (formulated in the essay of 1915) that exerts a continuing pressure on everything in conscious life; "repression proper," he states, is "actually an after-pressure" (XIV, 148). In the later writings, the dominance of the Death Instinct is implied in its silent working. Eros, by contrast, is visible and energetic. In *Totem and Taboo*, the historical past works through distortion and indirection and therefore silently and unconsciously. This metaphorical representation is consistent with the later idea that the organized and, therefore, observable emotions belong to the ego.

A large body of commentary exists to tell us that Freud's thinking on matters of anthropology was defective. It is customary to refer to *Totem and Taboo* as myth, though a few investigators have sought verification of its premises and conclusions.[2] Nevertheless the contribution of the work to Freud's thought was an essential one, for it provided the model by which external imperatives were to be established argumentatively. In *Totem and Taboo* that imperative is the historical reality which stands behind modern religion and other institutions. *The Future of an Illusion* would speak of Reason and Necessity (Logos and Ananke) in exactly such a frame of reference.

Toward the end of his brief discussion of tragedy, Freud defines "tragic guilt" as "the guilt which [the hero] had to take on himself in order to relieve the Chorus from theirs." (XIII, 156) And he states toward the end of the work:

It is not accurate to say that obsessional neurotics, weighed down under the burden of an excessive morality, are defending themselves only against *psychical* reality and are punishing themselves for impulses which were merely *felt*. Historical reality has a share in the matter as well. (XIII, 160–61)

These statements mark the transition to categorical statements about objective reality. In the final pages of *Totem and Taboo*, the analogical method of reasoning becomes a form of deduction, with the collapse of analogy into a single categorical proposition.

II   Group Psychology and the Analysis of the Ego

The implications of *Totem and Taboo* for a theory of art were left undeveloped, for the discussion of tragedy occupies about two pages. In *Group Psychology* (1921) Freud dealt with art at greater length—and with a topic of more vital interest to him, the institutions of religion. "Cruelty and intolerance towards those who do not belong to it are natural to every religion," he suggested

(XVIII, 98). His analysis of group psychology is perhaps his most definitive statement on the limits of personal freedom, essential to understanding his tragic conception of man and the peculiar effect that religion has on human life.

That analysis is introduced through a consideration of the ideas of Le Bon (*Psychology of Crowds*, 1895) and McDougall (*The Group Mind*, 1920). Le Bon had stressed suggestibility, the contagiousness of ideas, the magical power of words, and the role of illusion in the formation of crowd psychology, but it was his stress on the dominance of unconscious processes, accounting for the impulsiveness and irritability of crowds, that most impressed Freud. He was similarly impressed by McDougall's consideration of the intellectual inferiority promoted by groups, the result in part of the "intensification of affect" that group life promotes; "great decisions in the realm of thought and momentous discoveries and solutions of problems are only possible to an individual working in solitude," Freud states (XVIII, 83). His own theory is essentially a revision of McDougall's:

The problem consists in how to procure for the group precisely those features which were characteristic of the individual and which are extinguished in him by the formation of the group. For the individual, outside the primitive group, possessed his own continuity, his self-consciousness, his traditions and customs, his own particular functions and position, and he kept apart from his rivals. (XVIII, 86)

Through comparison of two markedly different groups, the church and the army, Freud emphasizes the attachment of libido to the leader and to the group. Representatives of either may be loved to such an extent that they possess the ego entirely and displace the conscience or ego ideal. In Freud's words, "A primary group of this kind is a number of individuals who have put one and the same object in the place of their ego-ideal and have consequently identified themselves with one another in their ego" (XVIII, 116). This process is a regressive one, since the individual returns to the pattern of early parental identifications in forming a relationship to the group. Intolerance and cruelty are, of course, manifestations of infantile organizations. Crowd behavior is infantile behavior, Freud implies.

He drew on *Totem and Taboo* for insights into the meaning of history and art, extending his terms in such a way that the frame of reference was single. Man need not think of evolving into the Nietzschean superman, he suggests, for he was superman at the beginning of history. This reference is not merely analogous, for comparisons, as we saw, are now propositions. Rejecting Trotter's "herd instinct" for the definition of man as a "horde animal," he suggests that the group is a "revival of the primal horde," the infantile prototype of the race (XVIII, 123). A modern phenomenon like hypnotism could be explained genetically. Hypnotism is thus a revitalization of the original relation to the father, through archaic inheritance; in psychoanalytic terms, the revitalization of a "passive-masochistic attitude" (XVIII, 127). "The leader of the group is still the dreaded primal father; the group still wishes to be governed by unrestricted force; it has an extreme passion for authority."

The main premise underlying this analysis—and, as we have seen, Freud's theory of art—is that interactions between the individual and any group (even the interaction of the analyst with his patient, forming a group of two) is invariably subrational. This is true of the transference on which therapy depends for its success, and the subrational identifications of art, largely inaccessible to literary analysis, depend on their remaining unexpressed.[3] In the identification of the epic poet—the prototype of the artist —with the hero of his own work, Freud was presenting a special version of the modern *persona*.[4]

In *Moses and Monotheism* Freud would indicate that epic poems are grounded in the mythology of a golden age, the memory of which undergoes repression during the latency period of the race. The reestablishment of the Mosaic religion, following the long worship of many gods during Jewish history, meant the restoration of the father ideal—the institution of the early parental imago as the group "object," as he had defined it in this monograph. *Group Psychology* suggests that the epic poet was the first to free himself from the horde through his imagination; indeed, he took over the role of the primal father:

This poet disguised the truth with lies in accordance with his longing. He invented the heroic myth. The hero was a man who by himself had slain the father—the father who still appeared in the myth as a totemic monster. Just as the father had been the boy's first ideal, so in the hero who aspires to the father's place the poet now created the first ego ideal. (XVIII, 136)

The favorite of the mother, the youngest son, probably makes transition to the hero possible; for he had been the father's replacement. Freud also suggests that the woman, who had tempted the brothers to commit murder, was in ancient poetry "probably turned into the active seducer and instigator to the crime."

In expressing this longing in a way by which an audience can identify with or seek their own lost childhood and murdered father, the poet becomes heroic:

> For he goes and relates to the group his hero's deeds which he has invented. At bottom this hero is no one but himself. Thus he lowers himself to the level of reality, and raises his hearers to the level of imagination. But his hearers understand the poet, and, in virtue of their having the same relation of longing towards the primal father, they can identify themselves with the hero. (XVIII, 136–37)

Art thus plays a dual role: in liberating the individual from the group through the agency of myth and in binding him to new identifications through imposition of an ego ideal to which an immense load of guilt may be attached and renewed periodically, even if assuaged through ritual and confession.

Freud's recognition of this dual process is part of the explanation for his ambivalence toward the social role of the artist. His intuition resembles that of Plato: the artist is the enemy of the rational life; for imagination and neurosis are related in mysterious ways. Freud's positive view of art is grounded in the belief that the insights of the artist are individual and never group achievements. This is one implication of Freud's concern with the intellectual inferiority of group life. But the price of intellectual achievement is often loneliness and inner stress, particularly where artistic sublimation weakens and neurosis supervenes (as in the case of Leonardo). These are states of mind unknown to those who have identified their will and desires with the group.

The ambiguity of Freud's attitude toward the artist is evident in this statement on art in the 1913 essay, "The Claims of Psychoanalysis to Scientific Interest":

> The artist's first aim is to set himself free and, by communicating his work to other people suffering from the same arrested desires, he offers them the same liberation. He represents his most personal wishful phantasies as fulfilled; but they only become a work of art when they have

undergone a transformation which softens what is offensive in them, conceals their personal origin and, by obeying the laws of beauty, bribes other people with a bonus of pleasure. (XIII, 187)

Each of these ideas has been taken as the Freudian esthetic; but though each is fundamental, each is dependent on the conception of the artist as simultaneously the primal father and "suffering servant" who redeems the group through his personal sacrifice. *Group Psychology* indirectly provides the mechanism by which this achievement of art is realized. The artist may himself become the "object" which gains possession of the ego:

Contemporaneously with this "devotion" of the ego to the object, which is no longer to be distinguished from a sublimated devotion to an abstract idea, the functions allotted to the ego ideal entirely cease to operate. The criticism exercised by that agency is silent; everything that the object does and asks for is right and blameless. (XVIII, 113)

III   The Future of an Illusion

Categorical propositions must after all conform to ordinary experience and reason: that is essentially the argument Freud uses against the impositions of religion in his chief statement on religion in his monograph of 1927. The illusions of religion might earlier have been dealt with by invoking the reality principle, but, as we have seen, the new instinctual theory had introduced a difficulty: man's destructiveness—the tendency in him to aggression—which works against cure. The resistance to truth was too great to insure the success of analysis. Might that not mean that nonrational solutions were best? This dilemma forced two strains of Freud's thought and temperament—his skepticism and his rationalism—into open debate. Since neither could show the way to reconciling experience with thought, it was necessary to allow each a voice and to see whether a balanced view or compromise might be effected. The monograph is thus written as a dialogue. As he had done in *The Question of Lay Analysis,* Freud employs a persona to express his skepticism—an opponent in an extended dialogue who questions the rationalism he wishes to invoke against religion and its institutions.

The impossibility of cure is stated early in the discussion:

"there are present in all men destructive, and therefore anti-social and anti-cultural, trends," and this is one reason that civilization is "built up on coercion and renunciation of instinct" (XXI, 7). The dominance of some men over others is therefore a necessity, and there must be, and are, agencies that seek to reconcile man to his culture nonrationally. Art does so through the social identification made possible through shared emotional experience; religion, by binding man to a "universal neurosis" (XXI, 44).

Up to this point experience has been speaking—including the experience of psychoanalysis with obsessional neurosis, which provides the analogical characterization of religion as "a system of wishful illusions together with a disavowal of reality, such as we find in an isolated form nowhere else but in amentia, in a state of blissful hallucinatory confusion" (XXI, 43). It is this "confusion" that permits the introduction of the rational intellect. As in analysis, the "effects of repression"—the teachings of religion based on "historical residues"—must be undone. Though Freud does not say so directly, the reason is implied: the obsessional neurotic—the religion-haunted man—is incapable of performing the work of civilization. The shift in emphasis has been gradual but it is momentous; it is the health of a civilization that matters. "Men cannot remain children for ever; they must in the end go out into 'hostile life' " (XXI, 49). They must be educated to reality. The solution to the impasse created by the destructive trends is to locate the reality principle in society: to erect it as an external necessity or imperative.

Simple observation shows that man's capacity for destructive behavior and unhappiness resists even the impositions of religion, which could achieve submission only through permitting sin and offering forgiveness in the name of a God who alone is good and capable of being so. But rationalism has had no better success: men accept the findings of science without accepting the scientific spirit and its ideal of man. Freud thus allows his skeptical opponent—or self—to ask a question toward which his thinking in this decade had been leading:

On the one hand you admit that men cannot be guided through their intelligence, they are ruled by their passions and their instinctual demands. But on the other hand you propose to replace the affective basis of their obedience to civilization by a rational one. . . . To me it seems that it must be either one thing or the other. (XXI, 46)

The solution that Freud proposes is evolutionary. And the trend of thought we have been concerned with throughout this study—the reification of instinctual forces into imperatives—is now fully and consciously articulated. The gods, Freud indicates, were themselves subject to Fate and hence became agents of redemption beyond this life. Their promise, in others words, is release from the fate of character—psychoanalytically, from repression and neurosis:

The notion dawned on the most gifted people of antiquity that Moira stood above the gods and that the gods themselves had their own destinies. And the more autonomous nature became and the more the gods withdrew from it, the more earnestly were all expectations directed to the third function of the gods—the more did morality become their true domain. (XXI, 18)

The intellect desires "the love of man and the decrease of suffering," but these can come about only as "external reality" —necessity—permits them to:

Our god [Logos] is perhaps not a very almighty one, and he may only be able to fulfill a small part of what his predecessors have promised. If we have to acknowledge this we shall accept it with resignation. (XXI, 54)

This, in brief, is Freud's answer to the question posed: both religion and science agree on the aims of life—universal love and a decrease in suffering—but it is plain that religion works against these even in the present. For if God alone is powerful and good, and man "weak and sinful," religion deals with instinctual demands by instituting further repression and directing the energies of mankind away from the solutions of the problems of living and toward sin and expiation as a means to achieving happiness in the next world. Culture thus exists on a precarious foundation. Only one solution is possible, and that is the power of intellect and science to eradicate ignorance. Only in religion do people defend ignorance and "rest content with such feeble grounds" for their opinions. And Freud adds: "Where questions of religion are concerned, people are guilty of every possible sort of dishonesty and intellectual misdemeanor" (XXI, 32). If the laws necessary to human society were freed from their alleged supernatural sanction, mankind would understand that they are intended to serve life, would become reconciled to them, and would seek to improve them, decreasing the pressures of civilized life.

Only reason can be depended on; a reason that is identical with science that can gain "some knowledge about the reality of the world" (XXI, 55). Though Freud is not concerned with the Kantian limits imposed on reason, he is consistent with Kant in arguing that inner feeling is unreliable as a guide to moral experience, and to objective reality as well, because it speaks differently to people.

These conclusions seem more positive than those considered in the later "Analysis Terminable and Interminable" only because religion as an alternative to the fallible reason is so undesirable. The "voice of the intellect" is that consciousness which permits man to sustain himself between importunate instinctual urges and external imperatives that would seem to bind him to Necessity. Freedom is the achievement of tragic awareness without the promise of solution.

IV Moses and Monotheism

The inquiry of *Totem and Taboo* into the origins of religion was completed in *Moses and Monotheism*, begun in Vienna in 1934 and completed in London in 1938. The work was thus symbolic of Freud's entry into exile, as the 1914 essay on the Moses of Michelangelo had unconsciously symbolized, perhaps, his situation with regard to those who had defected from psychoanalysis. But more significantly, Freud, in exploring the origins of anti-Semitism and the nature of modern Christian civilization, was declaring his allegiance to his persecuted brethren, an act comparable in spirit and intent to Arnold Schoenberg's in his work of the same period, the magnificent opera *Moses und Aron*.[5]

To be a Jew is not necessarily to have declared a belief in God: that is the major theme of *Moses and Monotheism*. Through an "instinctual renunciation" Judaism had dematerialized its God and surrendered the sensuality that marked the ancient religions of the mother goddess. It had given up myth, magic, sorcery, demonology. It differed from Christianity, then, in its wholly intellectual view of life and in the primacy of its ethical prescriptions. How this had come about Freud was uncertain. The root explanation could not be the advance of the patriarchal or masculine principle over the matriarchal, for it was the advance itself that made the accession of paternal authority possible. As in all situations in which sensuality is overcome, men perhaps "simply pronounce that what is more difficult is higher, and their pride is merely their narcissism augmented by the consciousness of a difficulty overcome" (XXIII, 118).

Freud based his interpretation of Moses on the "average legend" of the hero of Otto Rank.[6] In brief, the parents of the hero are aristocratic, usually royal in lineage. The conception of the hero is beset with great difficulties, the mother perhaps suffering a long period of barrenness. Before his birth, the parents receive a warning, through a dream or from an oracle, that the child to be born will endanger the father. At birth, therefore, the child is abandoned, usually in a basket set afloat in a river. He is rescued and brought up by animals or by a humble family, sometimes shepherds. When he reaches manhood, he discovers the identity of his true parents, revenges himself on his father or whoever ordered his abandonment, and after achieving the recognition due him becomes a great and famous man.

Moses departs from this pattern in being the child of humble people (Israelites) rather than of the royal house of Egypt, where he grew up. Drawing on his discoveries about the "family romance," Freud indicates that in everyday phantasy the family which exposes the child is invariably the imagined one, and the family which rescues him the real. This evidence suggests that Moses was actually an Egyptian, transposed into an Israelite. The transposition was necessary to make him heroic to the people for whom the legend was preserved. Though the hero normally rises from a humble station, the keynote of the Moses legend is that the hero steps down from a high position to serve a humble and persecuted people.

Freud based his theory on the writings of James Breasted, Eduard Meyer, and Ernst Sellin on the Egyptian pharaoh Akhenaten, the historical Moses, and related topics. From these speculations he drew the conclusion that monotheism originated with Akhenaten (d. 1358 B.C.), whose effort to displace the old polytheistic religion with the exclusive worship of a universal god associated with the life-giving sun came to an abrupt end with his death.[7] Moses was a royal official, perhaps the governor of

Goshen, who had been a follower of Akhenaten while he lived. He was acquainted with the Semitic people living in the frontier community, and in an effort to preserve the new religion he became their leader, instructed them in circumcision (an Egyptian custom) as a means of instilling in them a sense of their superiority, and led them out of Egypt (between 1358 and 1350 B.C.). Their destination was Canaan, occupied by Aramean tribes called the Habiru—a name which the followers of Moses eventually adopted. In an area south of Palestine, in what is now the Negev, the Israelites joined the worshippers of a volcano god, Yahweh, a cruel demon who roamed the area by night, and whose worship was instituted by a second Moses, son-in-law of the Midianite priest Jethro. The Israelites and Habiru united their gods. Yahweh became the liberator of the Israelites from Egypt; and the true liberator, the Egyptian Moses, was compensated by being put in the place of the Midianite priests. He was in fact united with the son-in-law of Jethro into the figure of the single law-giver.

Yahweh thus took on the ethical character of the Egyptian god of Akhenaten and Moses, yet retained some of his former qualities. During the forty years spent in the wilderness, the Jews murdered their harsh leader who had demanded their strict obedience. Following his death, polytheism came to dominate the life of the people, but the Mosaic tradition was preserved orally. Once this "latency" period ended, the Mosaic religion was re-established:

The remarkable fact with which we are here confronted is, however, that these traditions, instead of becoming weaker with time, became more and more powerful in the course of centuries, forced their way into the later revisions of the official accounts and finally showed themselves strong enough to have a decisive influence on the thoughts and actions of the people. (XXIII, 69)

The only explanation for this fact is the lingering guilt over the primal murder of the founder of the religion. The older epic tradition, Freud speculates, provided the materials of an epic literature, as in other cultures, commemorating a "golden age," the childhood world of a race. Later, Paul defined this lingering guilt as "original sin." Christianity substituted the "phantasy of atonement" described in *Totem and Taboo*, the sacrifice and eventual triumph of the "son" who was himself guiltless yet symbolized the ringleader of the primal horde. This phantasy became the gospel of redemption. Christ, then, was "the resurrected Moses" (XXIII, 90). With his substitution for God the Father and the institution of borrowed rituals and mystical ideas, and the reinstitution of the mother goddess, Christianity suffered a cultural "regression," for it was no longer monotheistic (XXIII, 88).

To this regression Freud attributes a number of causes of anti-Semitism, including the belief that the Jews carry the guilt of deicide and jealousy of the "chosen" first born. Circumcision is a chief cause, a reminder of the fear of castration of early days. But Freud had a more remarkable explanation for the contemporary persecutors of the Jews in Germany and Austria:

all those peoples who excel today in their hatred of Jews became Christians only in late historic times, often driven to it by bloody coercion. It might be said that they are all "misbaptized."

Under a "thin veneer of Christianity," they worship a "barbarous polytheism" as their ancestors had:

They have not got over a grudge against the new religion which was imposed on them; but they have displaced the grudge on to the source from which Christianity reached them.

The situation in Germany and Austria was thus a profoundly ironic one, for hatred of the Jews

is at bottom a hatred of Christians, and we need not be surprised that in the German National-Socialist revolution this intimate relation between the two monotheist religions finds such a clear expression in the hostile treatment of both of them. (XXIII, 91–92)

Moses had given the ancient Jews a supreme self-confidence, reflected in the optimism of their modern counterparts. To account for the persistence of these characteristics, Freud drew on the theory of acquired characteristics and inherited memory traces, to which he had alluded often in previous writings. Themes of this nature come together in an interpretation of modern Judaism, whose ethical prescriptions and *Weltanschauung* are implicitly those of psychoanalysis.

The confident declaration of faith in rationality, in *Future of an*

Illusion, had not been accounted for fully; it had merely been affirmed. Intellect earlier had been a tentative kind of reality testing in the service of the pleasure principle. *Moses and Monotheism* suggests that it might after all be an inherited state of mind: an ego ideal fostered by the memory of a long-dead heroic figure. A religion that departs from the rational prescriptions of a life-giving philosophy is regressive and bound to be ridden with superstition and sensuality, Freud continued to insist. In this conception of rationality and the theory of its formation, he had given psychoanalysis the underpinning of a mythology.

V   Civilization and Its Discontents

Corresponding with Einstein in 1932 on the problem of war, Freud wondered whether every science does not in the end arrive at "a kind of mythology" (XXII, 211). He uses the same phrase again in the *New Introductory Lectures* in reference to the theory of instincts "which is so to say our mythology" (XXII, 95). The effect of his new thinking on life and death led, as we have seen, to a view of man that could be related to a struggle between opposing forces in man and outside him—identified in "Analysis Terminable and Interminable" with the Love and Strife of Empedocles. *Moses and Monotheism* would complete this story by showing the descent of man—the creature of neurosis—from the killers of the primal father. The mythology of psychoanalysis is one finally concerned with the nature of death itself.

Death had been a major theme of Freud's writing at least from the outbreak of World War I. The great "Mourning and Melancholia," one of his most profound writings, belongs to this period. "Thoughts for the Times on War and Death," written in 1915, like the short essay on transience of the same year, is figurative and balanced in its prose, an unusual departure from the plain style of the contemporaneous essays on metapsychology. Freud's description of an older cosmopolitan and now displanted view of life is typical of the whole essay:

. . . he enjoyed the blue sea and the grey; the beauty of snow-covered mountains and of green meadow lands; the magic of northern forests and the splendor of southern vegetation; the mood evoked by landscapes that recall great historical events, and the silence of untouched nature. (XIV, 277)

The old civilized conventions of war, too, had passed, leading Freud to hope that Germany would prove to have broken the fewest of the agreements governing warfare, and leading him to express his disillusionment with mankind. He noted "the want of insight shown by the best intellects, their obduracy, their inaccessibility to the most forcible arguments and their uncritical credulity towards the most disputable assertions" (XIV, 287).

Surveying the progress of man's instinctual development, he concludes that there is no simple answer to the problem of good and evil, indeed there is "no such thing as 'eradicating' evil" (XIV, 281). For reason and intelligence are a mask for the passions which prove that man is a natural killer:

The very emphasis laid on the commandment 'Thou shalt not kill' makes it certain that we spring from an endless series of generations of murderers, who had the lust for killing in their blood, as, perhaps, we ourselves have today. (XIV, 296)

His only hope in 1915 was that admitting death into consciousness and ceasing to try to exist (through the agency of war) as "heroes who cannot believe in their own death" would somehow alleviate the circumstances that stamp "strangers as enemies, whose death is to be brought about or desired." Though admitting the reality of death might seem a regressive act, it was also the admission of truth: "To tolerate life remains, after all, the first duty of all living beings. Illusion becomes valueless if it makes this harder for us" (XIV, 299). The ideal community, he wrote Einstein seventeen years later, would be the "dictatorship of reason" (XXII, 213). Perhaps there might be hope for mankind, given the "constitutional intolerance of war" (XXII, 215).

Freud brought these themes together in the last of his major philosophical writings and the most important, *Civilization and Its Discontents* (1930). The structure of ideas which we have been tracing is completed here, though major themes were developed further in the last decade. Freud's major theme is that the original unity of ego and the external world gradually shrinks as man surrenders the pleasure principle for the reality principle; man is thus a diminished being, ridden with conflicts that civilization heightens rather than alleviates, not the creature of unlimited potentiality whose natural instincts are sources of happiness. There can be no Wordsworthian return through the imagination; man does not feel the pleasure of infancy again with "joy." The return, if it is made, is at the price of the present real world—the most valuable thing man has to lose.[8]

Freud begins by suggesting that the so-called "oceanic feeling" which his friend Romain Rolland had suggested was evidence of a religious dimension in life is only an intuition of that original unity between the ego and the world. If there is a purpose to life, it can only be "the program of the pleasure principle" (XXI, 76), and the thrust of the analysis is to show that the means of achieving pleasure—intoxication, sublimation, mass delusions like religion—are either not understood sufficiently to be greatly effective or are open to a privileged few only, or increase unhappiness instead of decreasing it. Religion diminishes the value of life instead of enhancing it, and misrepresents life delusionally (XXI, 84). Art is equally ineffective, for its "mild narcosis" offers only temporary relief from the miseries of living. Even the sense of beauty arises from inhibition of the sexual impulse, with the result that primary sexual characteristics are highly valued but are thought ugly, whereas secondary characteristics are thought beautiful. It is useless to seek to define happiness, even by comparison with other states of mind or other civilizations:

No matter how much we may shrink with horror from certain situations—of a galley-slave in antiquity, of a peasant during the Thirty Years' War, of a victim of the Holy Inquisition, of a Jew awaiting a pogrom—it is nevertheless impossible for us to feel our way into such people—to divine the changes which original obtuseness of mind, a gradual stupefying process, the cessation of expectations, and cruder or more refined methods of narcotization have produced upon their receptivity to sensations of pleasure and unpleasure. (XXI, 89)

The major part of the discussion is devoted to the argument that civilization is built upon a restriction of interests and gratifications—on the diminishment of the ego. The requirement of a single form of sexual life—heterosexual and monogamous—means that a large number of people are denied sexual gratification. There is for mankind, in fact, a denial of one half of one's sexual being, though Freud concedes that there is "something in the nature of the function itself which denies us full satisfaction and urges us along other paths" (XXI, 105). But more seriously, civilization promotes the illusion that humankind is gentle and loving and ignores their unloving aggressiveness. It refuses to recognize that the greater the demand for love of neighbor, the greater the aggressiveness humankind manifests. The internalization of aggression through the punishing superego means that the virtuous man is invariably unhappier than the sinner because continuous frustration promotes temptation. Indeed every instinctual renunciation as a rule increases the severity of conscience. Civilized man is self-ridden with guilt; his institutions are not the causes of neurosis but its products: "the inclination to aggression is an original, self-subsisting instinctual disposition in man, and . . . it constitutes the greatest impediment to civilization," Freud concludes (XXI, 122).

Civilization and Its Discontents is the most definitive expression of the tragic conception toward which Freud's thought was evolving; a vision without compensation or relief, for all avenues to an easing of anxiety or to the reconciliation are shown to be closed. By definition man is the creature of imbalance, not only between the environment and conflicting instincts, but between the instincts themselves. Where, as in other species, a balance is achieved, "a cessation of development" occurs (XXI, 123). It is this capacity for development and absence of solution—conflict itself—that ennobles man. Consciousness and thought are responses to stress and ambivalence, so that the more intense man's consciousness of his situation, and the more thoughtful his perception, the more unhappy he must be.

Freud's vision of man is, in the general sense of the word, existential. The original concern to provide psychology with a biological underpinning gave way to other interests, culminating in the effort to place man in a universal scheme of existence. He is ultimately conceived as the creature of imbalance and conflict, all of his achievements arising from perpetually contending, irreconcilable forces. Neurosis is no longer the disease of the traumatized or imperfectly mature individual: it is the condition of individual achievement and culture, the defining and special characteristic of mankind.

The achievement of this monumental essay is that Freud had come to recognize the tensions of his thought and its intellectual consequences and had voiced them without seeking to diminish either pessimism or harshness. The dialectical style had now resolved itself into the reflective. In characterizing man, Freud was characterizing himself; more so than *Moses and Monotheism*, the work is his late intellectual autobiography, the writing of which permitted him to achieve the eloquence and intellectual clarity of the late theoretical writings. Freud's major achievement as a writer was the expression of scientific discovery as intellectual autobiography and self-revelation—the dramatizing of a heroic persona whose tensions of mind are caught in every page.

CHAPTER 8

Conclusion

A most important statement on Freud's achievement as a writer
is that of Thomas Mann, in his tribute on the occasion of
Freud's eightieth birthday in 1936. Noting that Freud had developed his ideas independently of Nietzsche, Novalis, Kier-
kegaard, and Schopenhauer, and indeed had derived advantage
from unfamiliarity with ideas strongly resembling his own, Mann
nevertheless placed Freud in the main tradition of nineteenth-
century European thought. The main theme of that tradition,
Mann states, is the

confrontation of object and subject, their mingling and identification, the
resultant insight into the mysterious unity of ego and actuality, destiny
and character, doing and happening, and thus into the mystery of reality
as an operation of the psyche. . . .[1]

We have seen that Freud's characteristic solution to various problems in many areas of thought was the discovery of identities,
whether between inner and external imperatives and forces or
between author and spectator (hence the strongly rhetorical cast
and the most significant feature of his thinking on art). Furthermore, Freud's characteristic style is an outcome of this confrontation between object and subject: it is essentially, Mann states, an
"analytic revelation" that seeks to infiltrate thought and destroy
its naivete from within:

[It] takes from it the strain of its own ignorance, de-emotionalizes it, as it
were, inculcates the taste for understatement, as the English call it—for
the deflated rather than for the inflated words, for the cult which exerts
its influence by moderation, by modesty.[2]

146

Mann, in these words, has identified the dialectical style and the reflective with which we have been concerned in this study—and has indicated their relationship. Freud, I have tried to show, joins the great nineteenth-century tradition in his perception of a spiritual universe as noble and grand as the classical and the Christian. This older tradition identified the psyche with consciousness and thereby centered the distinctively human in rational awareness. But if the distinctively human was in a rationality arising from psychical disequilibrium and illness, then scientific discourse was no longer, and could no longer be, an exposition of ideas divorced from an account of their genesis. We have seen that the dialectical and reflective modes of discourse allowed Freud to realize these aims. He was able, in perfecting these modes, to humanize reason—to give it personal significance denied to it, as John Wren-Lewis has indicated—by the classical and Christian view which, in exalting the intellect, had "implied the insignificance of all merely personal considerations before the laws of the Great System of the World."[3] The dethronement of logic and the increasing emphasis on experimentation, in the empirical scientists and thinkers of the Enlightenment at least, was indirectly a declaration of faith in man's indispensable contribution to knowledge of the world.

Science henceforth began with man the perceiver and consequently man the thinker: the demonstration that perception was the inseparable partner of thought was the achievement of Descartes' *Discourse on Method*, and the point was not lost on those who followed him. Toward the end of the eighteenth century Immanuel Kant worked out its implications in his *Critique of Pure Reason*: the necessary proof of any existence apart from our own depends, Kant states in a passage on Descartes, on showing

that we have *experience*, and not merely imagination of outer things; and this, it would seem, cannot be achieved save by proof that even our inner experience, which for Descartes is indubitable, is possible only on the assumption of outer experience.[4]

In other words, Kant was unwilling to accept the idealism of Descartes or Berkeley (as he interpreted their idealism) which asserted that existence apart from ourselves was incapable of demonstration or even impossible of conception. The unquestionable reality of our "inner experience" Kant analyzed as the potentiality of the mind for experience of the world, the famous "categories" which not only fitted the mind to know the world but at the same time testified to the reality of that world:

I am conscious of my own existence as determined in time. All determination of time presupposes something *permanent* in perception. This permanent cannot, however, be something in me, since it is only through this permanent that my existence in time can itself be determined.[5]

This, in brief, is the meaning of Mann's statement that in the nineteenth-century tradition subject and object were mingled and identified.

The intellectual faculties, Kant had shown also, were limited in what they could know. Man might distinguish the unity, the possibility, and the actuality of experience, but he could neither prove nor disprove through "pure" reason that God exists and that man has a free will and an immortal soul. These unknowable or, more exactly, "noumenal" ideas are necessary to our thinking about the world but are not guaranteed to exist by virtue of the power to think. There might be, however, something else in man that testified to their reality, chiefly his freedom or will to act on ideas given by his reason: man is free when he acts as a free man. But Kant was not saying that feeling or will or consciousness were themselves sources of truth. He sought to deal with this question in his later writings, and his successors—dissatisfied with his answers or misunderstanding his sometimes inconsistent words —sought to restore to man the fullness of perception and knowledge that Kant had denied him. "The intellect searches out the absolute order of things as they stand in the mind of God," Emerson wrote in 1836, "and without the colors of affection." There was in the phrase of Thomas Carlyle a "natural supernaturalism" whereby man pierces the "eternal" by looking into his own soul: "It is a mysterious indescribable process, that of getting to believe—indescribable, as all vital acts are. We have our mind given us, not that it may cavil and argue, but that it may see into something, given us clear belief and understanding about something, whereon we are then to proceed to act."[6] Whether conceived as Imagination (by William Blake) or as the Will or the "Higher Reason," this power of mind for the Romantic was absolute and unconditioned—indeed the primary reality.

Earlier we briefly considered the rival scientific traditions of the nineteenth century—the materialist and the vitalistic. The second of these traditions was promoted by the Romantic tradition of thought just characterized, though it did not originate in the Romantic movement; vitalistic ideas may be traced as far back as Aristotle. Freud, we have seen, was strongly influenced by the vitalistic tradition of the nineteenth century, though he was trained in the materialistic tradition. It was his reading of the essay on nature attributed to Goethe that inspired him to study medicine, he indicates in the autobiographical study.

Given the concern with the mysteriousness of human nature in the vitalistic tradition and in the voluntarist thought of Schopenhauer, Nietzsche, and others, it is not coincidental that Mann puts most stress on Freud's discovery of the id —characterized by Mann (citing the *New Introductory Lectures*) as "a chaos, a melting-pot of seething excitations."[7] For the id is the reservoir, the embodiment of the quintessentially mysterious in man. The vitalistic strain in Freud's thought is realized in the id—its formulation grounded not in directly observed, measurable experience but in a deduction deriving from the problematic nature of consciousness and the unconscious. The id finally was the source of those imperatives—those vital forces—that joined inner with external experience. Consistent with the post-Kantian Romantic philosophers, Freud redefined rational awareness to take account of feeling. Indeed the mysteriousness of feeling itself is the central unstated theme of his life's work. Whatever name may be given to the complexes and traits of characters, the passions are mysterious and remain so.

But owing to his background and training, Freud sought that redefinition within a frame of discourse that would give due recognition to experimentation and inductive science. As I have suggested, it was Mill—particularly the essays on religion—that Freud drew upon as a model of discourse. In his autobiography, perhaps the greatest written in the nineteenth century, Mill had shown himself as a man thinking and feeling; indeed his demonstration that feeling is the inseparable partner of perception and thought may have powerfully influenced the discourse that Freud perfected in *The Interpretation of Dreams, Psychopathology of Everyday Life*, and the case histories.

That discourse marks the transition in Freud to increasingly deductive modes of thought. It is worth pointing out in way of conclusion that the application of deductive methods to problems of psychology was no more unscientific than the deductive investigations such as Einstein conducted in his "thought experiments." Such methods are particularly common in science where empirical observations are not yet possible or the tools or methods of investigation are in dispute. Neutron stars were conceived as theoretical ideas before their discovery in the 1960's, and astronomers today seek the confirmation of theoretical "black holes"—exactly as scientists sought confirmation of Einstein's Special Theory in the eclipse of 1919. It begs the question, then, to attack Freudian ideas merely as "speculative" or purely "deductive." Freud himself demanded their verification in empirical investigation. What remained at issue at the time of his death —and continues to be at issue—is the method of investigation to be employed. Psychoanalytic methods continue to be debated, as numerous symposiums testify. As late as 1958, the distinguished Harvard physicist and philosopher of science, Percy W. Bridgman, commented:

in spite of the apparently unsatisfactory status of some of the constructs of the psychoanalyst it would appear that there is nothing fundamentally unsound at the foundations, but . . . if one takes the necessary trouble and care everything can be put on a completely "operational" basis—it is not necessary to postulate unprovable principles or essences such as the vitalist does, for example.

And he added perceptively that the decisive role of introspection distinguishes psychoanalysis from other sciences:

This role is fundamental, because without the introspectional report that the analyst is able to draw from his patient some of the basic concepts of the analyst are merely verbal constructs—they have no "reality" because there is no second method of getting to the terminus.[8]

The philosopher Raphael Demos, speaking at the same conference, chose to characterize psychoanalysis as a "protoscience," and further stated: "In its early stages as a science, such exercise of the speculative imagination is inevitable and may be useful."[9] It is not established or agreed upon, then, that Freudian psychology is either unfounded or outmoded: the scientific status of psychoanalysis, like that of psychology generally, remains controversial, and rival traditions are not yet in even approximate agreement on basic premises and methods.

What is not in dispute is Freud's immense influence on the culture of our time. And his place in world literature seems assured. W. H. Auden, in his great memorial poem on Freud, refers to his "technique of unsettlement" that attacked the "ancient cultures of conceit." As scientist and writer, Freud joined his predecessors who understood that progress meant standing against the "compact majority" and its unexamined moral assumptions. His allegiance throughout his life was to those philosophers of science who perpetuated the spirit of the Enlightenment, though discarding some of its scientific ideas and world picture. His particular achievement was to exhibit, in Auden's phrase, the "richness of feeling" in the act of thought itself.

Notes and References

Preface

1. *Essays* (New York: Knopf, 1957), p. 310.
2. *Freud: The Mind of the Moralist* (Garden City, New York: Anchor Books, 1961), pp. 16–17. Rieff argues that Freud's view of man is not finally tragic—a view contrary to the one I shall develop. In the sentences that follow I have drawn on his discussion of Freud's conception of instinct. Throughout this study I have drawn on Robert B. Heilman's analysis of tragedy, in his book *Tragedy and Melodrama: Versions of Experience* (Seattle: University of Washington Press, 1968).
3. "Love's Coming of Age," in Charles Rycroft, ed., *Psychoanalysis Observed* (Baltimore: Penguin Books, 1968), p. 87.
4. Robert R. Holt, "A Review of Some of Freud's Biological Assumptions and Their Influence on His Theories," in Norman S. Greenfield and William C. Lewis, eds., *Psychoanalysis and Current Biological Thought* (Madison and Milwaukee: University of Wisconsin Press, 1965), p. 100.

Chapter One

1. The facts stated in this chapter are taken from Ernest Jones, *The Life and Work of Sigmund Freud*, 3 vols. (New York: Basic Books, 1953, 1955, 1957), unless otherwise indicated.
2. Martin Freud, *Sigmund Freud: Man and Father* (New York: Vanguard Press, 1958), p. 11. Little is known about Freud's religious background. Earl A. Grollman comments on Freud's instruction in Hebrew, in *Judaism in Sigmund Freud's World* (New York: Appleton-Century, 1965), pp. 51–53. The fullest discussion of the background is in David Bakan, *Sigmund Freud and the Jewish Mystical Tradition* (Princeton: D.

C. Van Nostrand, 1958). See also Friedrich Heer, "Freud, the Viennese Jew," in Jonathan Miller, ed., *Freud: The Man, His World, His Influence* (Boston: Little, Brown, 1972), pp. 2–20.

3. Jones, III, 237; I, 31; I, 197; *Standard Edition*, XX, 274. Subsequent references in the text are to the *Standard Edition*.

4. Miller, p. 6.

5. Jones, II, 415; II, 22; Martin Freud, pp. 70–71.

6. Ernst L. Freud, ed., *Letters of Sigmund Freud* (London: Hogarth Press, 1970), pp. 85–86. Later quotations are from pp. 91, 297–98.

7. *Sigmund Freud*, p. 138.

8. Sigmund Freud, *The Origins of Psychoanalysis*, ed. M. Bonaparte, Ernst Kris, and Anna Freud (New York: Basic Books, 1954), p. 82. Freud's statements on Fliess are quoted by Jones, I, 302, 317.

9. *Origins*, p. 211.

10. Henrik M. Ruitenbeek, ed., *Freud As We Knew Him* (New York: Basic Books, 1973), p. 328.

11. Miller, pp. 9–10, 44.

12. *Origins*, p. 311.

13. William McGuire, ed., *The Freud/Jung Letters*, tr. Ralph Manheim and R. F. C. Hull (Princeton: Princeton University Press, 1974); March 8 and March 14, 1911.

14. Ibid., March 25, 1911.

15. Jones, II, 139.

16. Ernst Pfeiffer, ed., *Sigmund Freud and Lou Andreas-Salomé Letters* (New York: Harcourt Brace Jovanovich, 1966), p. 154.

17. Ernst L. Freud, ed., *The Letters of Sigmund Freud and Arnold Zweig* (New York: Harcourt Brace Jovanovich, 1970), p. 25.

18. Ruitenbeek, p. 366. On correspondences with Spinoza see A. A. Brill, in Ruitenbeek, p. 152; Abraham Kaplan, "Freud and Modern Philosophy," in Benjamin Nelson, ed., *Freud and the Twentieth Century* (New York: Meridian Books, 1957), pp. 209–29; Paul Ricoeur, *Freud and Philosophy*, tr. Denis Savage (New Haven: Yale University Press, 1970), p. 391.

19. Jones, III, 312–13. On the sources of Freud's evolutionary theory, see Abram Kardiner, "Social and Cultural Implications of Psychoanalysis," in Sidney Hook, ed., *Psychoanalysis, Scientific Method, and Philosophy* (New York: New York University Press, 1959), pp. 82–88.

20. Ruitenbeek, p. 94.

21. Ibid., p. 355.

22. *Letters*, pp. 295–96.

23. *Freud: The Mind of the Moralist*, p. 204.

24. Jones, II, 398. The medical history is found in Chapter 15 of this volume and Appendix B of Volume III.

25. Ibid., II, 417.

26. Although a psychoanalytic biography has not yet appeared, there have been important contributions by Jones and others to one. See Harry Slochower, "Freud's *Déjà Vu* on the Acropolis," *Psychoanalytic Quarterly*, 39 (1970), 90–102; Leonard Shengold, "Freud and Joseph," in Mark Kanzer, ed., *The Unconscious Today* (New York: International Universities Press, 1971), pp. 473–94.

27. Paul Roazen, *Freud: Political and Social Thought* (New York: Knopf, 1968), pp. 94–95.

Chapter Two

1. William P. D. Wightman, *The Growth of Scientific Ideas* (New Haven: Yale University Press, 1951), p. 382. A full account of Freud's predecessors is found in Jones, I, 41–43.

2. For important and representative criticism of these formulations, see the articles of B. A. Farrell in S. G. M. Lee and Martin Herbert, eds., *Freud and Psychology* (Baltimore: Penguin Books, 1970); Benjamin B. Rubinstein and Robert R. Holt, in Greenfield and Lewis; Lawrence S. Kubie, in E. Pumpian-Mindlin, ed., *Psychoanalysis as Science* (Stanford: Stanford University Press, 1952); Ernest Nagel, in Hook. For support of Freud's scientific method and definitions, see Herbert Weiner and Sydney G. Margolin, in Greenfield and Lewis, and Pumpian-Mindlin in *Psychoanalysis as Science*.

3. Heinz Hartmann comments that Freud's "concept of drives had to prove its usefulness with respect to human psychology. Here, the sources of the drives are of much less importance than their aims and their objects. The lesser rigidity of the human drives, the comparatively easy shift of the aims, the freeing of many activities from a rigid connection with one definite instinctual tendency, the comparative independence from and variety of possible response to outer and inner stimuli have to be taken into account in considering the role of the drives in human psychology." "Psychoanalysis as a Scientific Theory," in Hook, p. 11.

4. *Letters*, p. 392.

Chapter Three

1. Jones, I, 224; Freud, XIV, 11–12.

2. Freud later distinguished "substitute formations" that originate in the conscious or preconscious and are transformed into symptoms such as the reaction formations in obsessional neurosis. See XIV, 179.

3. Freud returned to paranoia in 1915, in a short case history concerned with female homosexuality, and in a case history of 1920 which deals at length with homosexuality and concludes that masculinity and femininity are impossible to define psychoanalytically and must be reserved to biological investigation (XVIII, 171).

4. The memoirs of the patient, accompanied by illustrations, a reprinting of Freud's history, and additional notes by the later analyst, Ruth Mack Brunswick, are found in Muriel Gardiner, ed., *The Wolf-Man* (New York: Basic Books, 1971).

5. Anthony Quinton, "Freud and Philosophy," in Miller, p. 72.

6. *Freud and Philosophy*, pp. 96, 107.

7. Ibid., p. 396.

Chapter Four

1. Stanley Edgar Hyman suggests that later images of exploration relate to the sexual exploration of a woman's body. *The Tangled Bank* (New York: Atheneum, 1962), pp. 333–35. Hyman also traces other patterns of imagery and notes the possible influence of Conan Doyle's Sherlock Holmes, first suggested by Theodor Reik.

2. Strachey summarizes the background of the essay in his introduction to it (III, 301–02). Screen memories are insignificant early events that are substituted for more important later ones (discussed in this essay), or the reverse, later insignificant events that substitute for early important ones. In a 1913 essay on dreams, Freud shows how fairy tales often serve as screen memories.

3. *Freud and Philosophy*, pp. 105, 110.

4. "What Makes Basic Research Basic?", in Richard Thruelson and John Kobler, eds., *Adventures of the Mind* (New York: Knopf, 1960), pp. 153–54.

5. Incidentally, the 1908 essay on sexual morality is a corrective to the view that Freud regarded woman as constitutionally inferior to men intellectually, though he does insist that women have less capacity for sublimation. Intellectual inferiority, he states, is probably owing to "the inhibition of thought necessitated by sexual suppression" (IX, 199).

6. *Freud: The Mind of the Moralist*, xiii.

7. Jones, II, 282.

8. Ricoeur deals exhaustively with correspondences between Freud and Kant, suggesting that Freud's recognition of affinities was not a superficial observation. See pp. 433–39.

Chapter Five

1. Rieff considers spontaneity of little importance in Freud's thinking (p. 386); Norman O. Brown gives it greater weight in *Life Against Death*

(Middletown, Conn.: Wesleyan University Press, 1959), pp. 59–61. Jack Spector argues that Freud stresses sublimation rather than catharsis, in *The Aesthetics of Freud* (New York: Praeger, 1972), p. 104.

2. Harry Slochower explores the biographical implications of the study in "Freud's *Gradiva*: Mater Nuda Rediviva," *Psychoanalytic Quarterly*, 40 (1971), 646–62.

3. Freud's translation of Leonardo's *nibio* ("kite") by "vulture" and other mistakes have provoked much negative comment. See Meyer Schapiro, "Leonardo and Freud: An Art-Historical Study," *Journal of the History of Ideas*, 17 (April, 1956), 147–78; and Spector, pp. 53–58.

4. Bullitt indicates in his foreword to the book that in 1932 Freud "made textual changes and wrote a number of new passages to which I objected," and that in 1938 he agreed to their deletion. The text gives the impression throughout of a palimpsest: a basic account of Wilson's life and career (presumably written by Bullitt), with additions interpreting Wilson's behavior. Sigmund Freud and William C. Bullitt, *Thomas Woodrow Wilson: A Psychological Study* (Boston: Houghton Mifflin, 1967), viii. Subsequent references appear in the text. Two important estimates of the book are those of Barbara Tuchman, "Can History Use Freud?" *Atlantic Monthly* (February, 1967), 40–44, and Paul Roazen, *Freud: Political and Social Thought*, pp. 300–32. Tuchman is critical of the historical assumptions and method but praises the insights into Wilson's neurosis. Roazen reviews the controversy over the book, notes important similarities between Wilson and Freud, and criticizes the absence of discussion of Wilson's social world: "One would have to establish very securely what the social conventions of the Reconstruction South were before one could claim to have understood what was idiosyncratic in what Wilson said or wrote" (p. 309).

5. Allen Tate, "Tension in Poetry," in *Reason in Madness: Critical Essays* (New York: G. P. Putnam's Sons, 1941), p. 71.

6. William K. Wimsatt, Jr., *The Verbal Icon* (Lexington: University of Kentucky Press, 1954), p. 81.

7. Ibid., p. 82.

8. T. S. Eliot, *Selected Essays* (New York: Harcourt Brace Jovanovich, 1950), p. 115.

9. "Bottom's Dream," *Virginia Quarterly Review*, 42 (1966), 556.

10. "Art and Neurosis," in William Phillips, ed., *Art and Psychoanalysis* (Cleveland: World Publishing Company, 1963), p. 517; *Psychoanalytic Explorations in Art* (New York: Schocken Books, 1964), p. 318. Spector discusses at length and in different terms Freud's attitude toward the "voluntary aspect of artistic 'illusion.'" *The Aesthetics of Freud*, pp. 134–35.

11. *The Dynamics of Literary Response* (New York: Oxford University Press, 1968), p. 102. For a penetrating analysis of recent "anaesthetic criticism," "a version using Freud's terminology but lacking Freud's sympathy for the way great artists court unconscious engulfment in order

to recreate the conditions of a human order," see Frederick Crews, in *Psychoanalysis and Literary Process* (Cambridge, Mass.: Winthrop Publishers, 1970), pp. 1–24.

Chapter Six

1. *Freud and Philosophy*, p. 293.

2. In "Dostoevsky and Parricide," Freud offers a somewhat different explanation of this phenomenon. Where a need for punishment develops in a masochistic ego and the superego is sadistic, the ego submits to "Fate": "For every punishment is ultimately castration and, as such, a fulfillment of the old passive attitude towards the father. Even Fate is, in the last resort, only a later projection of the father" (XXI, 185).

3. The will, for Schopenhauer, "dispenses altogether with a final goal and aim. It always strives, for striving is its sole nature, which no attained goal can put an end to." Through "knowledge of the whole," however, the will can renounce life: man can attain a state of "voluntary renunciation, resignation, true indifference, and perfect will-lessness." Irwin Edman, ed., *The Philosophy of Schopenhauer* (New York: Random House, 1928), pp. 248, 305.

4. Hyman, in *The Tangled Bank*, discusses other nineteenth- and twentieth-century scientific discourses that undoubtedly influenced Freud.

5. The influence of Schopenhauer may have been strong here too: "The intellect can do nothing more than bring out clearly and fully the nature of the motives; it cannot determine the will itself; for the will is quite inaccessible to it, and . . . cannot be investigated." *The Philosophy of Schopenhauer*, p. 233.

6. Hyman discusses the implications of these ideas for a theory of tragedy. "Psychoanalysis and the Climate of Tragedy," in Nelson, *Freud and the Twentieth Century*, pp. 167–85.

Chapter Seven

1. Numerous psychoanalytic theories of art have dealt with the form of the work in a way comparable to Freud's dealing with "petty ceremonials." Holland cites a number of them, including that of Franz Alexander who states: "The fusion of form and content is the essence of art. Form makes possible the gratification of a repressed wish because the emotional discharge is attributed to something acceptable—namely, to pleasure afforded by the form." *The Dynamics of Literary Response*, pp. 296–97. A most subtle and perhaps little-known theory is that of John

Rickman. In one of the phases of what he calls the "graphic impulse" of the child, "attention is paid to the depiction of the form of the external object, interest being driven to it perhaps through anxiety as to the fate of its inner counterpart, but the treatment of details is governed by part-object interests." "Ugliness and the Creative Impulse," in Hendrik M. Ruitenbeek, ed., *The Creative Imagination* (Chicago: Quadrangle Books, 1965), p. 112.

2. The most famous of the Freudian anthropologists is Géza Róheim. See his *The Origin and Function of Culture* (Garden City, New York: Anchor Books, 1971). Perhaps the most famous assessment of Freud's anthropological theory is that of A. L. Kroeber, in *The Nature of Culture* (Chicago: University of Chicago Press, 1952), pp. 301–309. The merits of Freud's theory are considered by Rieff in *Freud: The Mind of the Moralist*, Chapter 6, and L. A. White, *The Science of Culture* (New York: Farrar, Straus and Cudahy, 1949), Chapter XI. Also see Hyman, *The Tangled Bank*, p. 366.

3. A major theme of D. H. Lawrence, powerfully treated in his short novel *The Fox*. I have discussed this point in "The Symbolism of Lawrence's *The Fox*," *CLA Journal*, XI (1967), 135–41.

4. "As in the drama, as in fiction, the action of the lyric must function as a trope, a figure, a mask, an affirmation in symbolic terms of whatever it is that the poet, most deeply, is telling us. The speech of literature is different in kind from that of ordinary talk, and the lyric, no less than the drama, is a stylized abstraction of the human dialogue, not an instance of it." George Wright, *The Poet in the Poem* (Berkeley: University of California Press, 1962), p. 21.

5. See George Steiner's brief discussion of the similarity in *Language and Silence* (New York: Atheneum, 1967), p. 133.

6. Freud wrote "Family Romances" as an introduction to Rank's book on the hero in 1909. Less known but of equal interest and importance is Karl Abraham's essay of the same year, "Dreams and Myths," which concerns Prometheus, Moses, and other legendary figures. See his *Clinical Papers and Essays on Psychoanalysis* (London: The Hogarth Press, 1955), pp. 153–209.

7. Abraham published a long essay on Akhenaten in 1912. See "Amenhotep IV," in *Clinical Papers*, pp. 262–90. An important critique on the evidence gathered on Akhenaten—with passing reference to Freud—is the essay of L. A. White, "Ikhnaton: The Great Man vs. the Culture Process," in *The Science of Culture*, pp. 233–81. The evidence is also reviewed by Crane Brinton, *A History of Western Morals* (New York: Harcourt Brace Jovanovich, 1959), pp. 38–46.

8. The possibility of an unrepressed art and civilization is the subject of Norman O. Brown, *Life Against Death*, Chapters 5, 12, 16, and Herbert Marcuse, *Eros and Civilization* (New York: Vintage Books, 1955).

Chapter Eight

1. *Essays*, p. 304.

2. Ibid., p. 324.

3. *Psychoanalysis Observed*, pp. 86–87.

4. *Immanuel Kant's Critique of Pure Reason*, tr. Norman Kemp Smith (London: Macmillan, 1953), p. 244.

5. Ibid., p. 245.

6. *On Heroes, Hero-Worship and the Heroic in History* (London: Dent, 1908), p. 401. "Natural Supernaturalism" is discussed in *Sartor Resartus*.

7. *Essays*, p. 309.

8. Hook, *Psychoanalysis, Scientific Method, and Philosophy*, p. 282.

9. Ibid., pp. 329–30.

Selected Bibliography

BIBLIOGRAPHIES

The most complete bibliography is Alexander Grinstein, *The Index of Psychoanalytic Writings* (New York: International Universities Press, 1956—), a revision and updating of John Rickman, *Index Psycho-analyticus*, 1893–1926 (London: The Hogarth Press, 1926). The individual volumes of the *Standard Edition* (see below) contain valuable bibliographies. Articles and discussion of Freud can be located through the *Psychological Index* (1894–1935) and its successor, *Psychological Abstracts; Annual Survey of Psychoanalysis*, 10 vols. (1950–71); J. Bolland and J. Sandler, *The Hampstead Psychoanalytic Index* (New York: International Universities Press, 1965); *Literature and Psychology* annual bibliography (recently discontinued); N. Kiell, *Psychoanalysis, Psychology and Literature: A Bibliography* (Madison: University of Wisconsin Press, 1963). A few of the journals that publish important articles on Freud are *American Imago, Literature and Psychology, Psychoanalytic Quarterly, Psychoanalytic Review, International Journal of Psychoanalysis* (now the *International Review of Psychoanalysis*), *Psychiatric Quarterly*.

PRIMARY SOURCES

Letters of Sigmund Freud, 1873–1939. Edited by Ernst Freud. London: The Hogarth Press, 1970. Freud was one of the great letter writers, as this indispensable and well-edited collection shows. The engagement letters to Martha Bernays, short passages of which were printed by Jones, are included.

The Letters of Sigmund Freud and Arnold Zweig. Edited by Ernst Freud. New York: Harcourt Brace Jovanovich, 1970. An important correspondence beginning in 1927. Indispensable to an understanding of Freud's character and thought in the final decade.

The Origins of Psychoanalysis: Letters to Wilhelm Fliess, Drafts and Notes: 1877–1902. Edited by M. Bonaparte, Anna Freud and Ernst Kris. New York: Basic Books, 1954. Most of the 284 letters of Freud to Fliess, acquired by Marie Bonaparte and preserved through World War II, are included in this remarkable book, together with the "Scientific Project" of 1895. Basic to an understanding of Freud the man and the scientist in the 1890's.

The Standard Edition of the Complete Psychological Works. Edited by James Strachey, Anna Freud, Alix Strachey, and Alan Tyson. 24 vols. London: The Hogarth Press and The Institute of Psychoanalysis, 1954–74. A great achievement in translation and scholarship, providing the full text of certain works for the first time and superseding the inadequate Brill translations (in the Modern Library). In some of his translations Brill reduced the text and substituted his own examples (see VI, xi for discussion of these changes). Scholarly introductions tracing the course of Freud's thinking; full cross-references, footnotes, bibliographies. Some of the translations are modifications and revisions by earlier translators of the *Collected Papers* (1924–50) and volumes in the International Psychoanalytical Library. Comparison with these earlier renderings is often necessary to clarify certain ideas. A critique of the translation problems and their solution in the Standard Edition needs to be undertaken.

The Freud/Jung Letters: The Correspondence between Sigmund Freud and C. G. Jung. Edited by William McGuire. Translated by Ralph Manheim and R. F. C. Hull. Princeton: Princeton University Press, 1974. A correspondence as important to understanding Freud from 1907 to 1914 as the Fliess correspondence is to understanding the earlier Freud. Useful annotations.

Minutes of the Vienna Psychoanalytic Society. Edited by Herman Nunberg and Ernest Federn. 2 vols. New York: International Universities Press, 1962, 1967.

Sigmund Freud and Lou Andreas-Salomé Letters. Edited by Ernst Pfeiffer. New York: Harcourt Brace Jovanovich, 1966. Personal letters from the years of dissension with Jung to the 1930's.

SECONDARY SOURCES

I. Biography

ALEXANDER, FRANZ, EISENSTEIN, SAMUEL, GROTJAHN, MARTIN, eds. *Psychoanalytic Pioneers.* New York: Basic Books, 1966. Biographical studies of Abraham, Rank, Eitingon, Jones, and other men associated with Freud.

BROME, VINCENT. *Freud and His Early Circle*. London: Heinemann, 1967. A detailed study of the formative years of the psychoanalytic movement and of Freud's relations to Jung and others. Important discussion of Jung's alleged racial thinking and his connection with the Nazi movement. A necessary supplement to Jones.

EISSLER, K. R. *Talent and Genius*. New York: Quadrangle Books, 1971. Deals with the charge of plagiarism raised against Freud in his relations with the analyst Viktor Tausk (the subject of Paul Roazen's *Brother Animal*, 1969). A brilliant discussion of Freud the genius and of scientific discovery in general.

FREUD, MARTIN. *Sigmund Freud: Man and Father*. New York: Vanguard, 1958. Details of Freud's home life and personal character.

JONES, ERNEST. *The Life and Work of Sigmund Freud*. New York: Basic Books, 1953, 1955, 1957. The standard, official biography, respectful and partisan on controversial points. Encyclopedic account of Freud's scientific career and personal life; a diffuse but authoritative and plainly written account of the ideas and writings.

LOEWENBERG, PETER. "A Hidden Zionist Theme in Freud's 'My Son, The Myops . . .' Dream," *Journal of the History of Ideas*, 31 (1970), 129–32. Argues the thesis that Freud repressed his Zionist interests because he envied "Jewish salvation through politics." An important contribution to an understanding of Freud's Judaism.

McGRATH, WILLIAM J. "Student Radicalism in Vienna," *Journal of Contemporary History*, II, 3 (1967), 183–201. Freud, Herzl, and the radical political climate of the 1870's. Important to an understanding of the intellectual climate of Freud's university years.

MILLER, JONATHAN, ed. *Freud: The Man, His World, His Influence*. Boston: Little, Brown, 1972. Eleven essays on a range of topics, including Freud and Marx and his philosophical backgrounds. Three important essays by Friedrich Heer, George Rosen, and Martin Esslin on his Viennese background and medical experience.

RUITENBEEK, HENDRICK M., ed. *Freud As We Knew Him*. Detroit: Wayne State University Press, 1973. Characterizations and accounts of Freud and his career by colleagues, students, patients, and friends, including James Putnam, Adolph Stern, Joan Riviere, Franz Alexander, Helene Deutsch, Heinrich Racker, and Edoardo Weiss. Invaluable collection of source materials and bibliographies.

RYCROFT, CHARLES, ed. *Psychoanalysis Observed*. London: Constable, 1966. Important essays on the historical and cultural significance of psychoanalysis by Geoffrey Gorer, John Wren-Lewis, and others.

SACHS, HANNS. *Freud, Master and Friend*. Cambridge: Harvard University Press, 1944. Reminiscences and comments on Freud by an early disciple and colleague.

SCHUR, MAX. *Freud: Living and Dying*. New York: International Univer-

sities Press, 1972. Account of the Fliess years and Freud's long illness by the physician who attended him from 1929 to his death.
An important supplement to Jones.

SLOCHOWER, HARRY. "Freud's *Déjà Vu* on the Acropolis,"
Psychoanalytic Quarterly, 39 (1970), 90–102.

II. Scientific Ideas and Methods

BRENNER, CHARLES. *An Elementary Textbook of Psychoanalysis.* Revised edition. Garden City, New York: Anchor Books, 1974. A
lucid and well-organized exposition of psychoanalytic ideas. Ideal
for the beginning reader.

ELLENBERGER, HENRI F. *The Discovery of the Unconscious: The History
and Evolution of Dynamic Psychology.* New York: Basic Books,
1970. Freud as the heir of a long and distinguished line of
nineteenth-century dynamic psychologists instead of as a pioneering discoverer. Argues that hostility toward Freud has been exag-
gerated. "Much of what is credited to Freud was diffuse current
lore, and his role was to crystallize these ideas and give them an
original shape." Encyclopedic, frequently diffuse, important to an
assessment of Freud's scientific achievement.

FENICHEL, OTTO. *The Psychoanalytic Theory of Neurosis.* New York:
W. W. Norton and Company, 1945. A rewriting and expansion of
the still valuable *Outline of Clinical Psychoanalysis*, 1934. The
most complete account available of psychoanalytic theory, incor-
porating the theories and clinical findings of analysts up to 1945. A
synthetic rather than critical or analytic work.

GARDINER, MURIEL, ed. *The Wolf-Man.* New York: Basic Books, 1971.
The memoirs of the "wolf man," together with Freud's great 1918
case history and additional notes by Ruth Mack Brunswick who
treated the patient later.

GREENFIELD, NORMAN S. and LEWIS, WILLIAM C. eds. *Psychoanalysis and
Current Biological Thought.* Madison and Milwaukee: University
of Wisconsin Press, 1965. An important collection of essays on the
methods and biological assumptions of psychoanalysis.

HOOK, SIDNEY, ed. *Psychoanalysis, Scientific Method, and Philosophy.*
New York: New York University Press, 1959. An important collec-
tion of essays on the language and philosophical assumptions of
psychoanalysis by a number of important writers, including Heinz
Hartmann, Ernest Nagel, Abram Kardiner, and Morris Lazerowitz.
The Lazerowitz essay is highly recommended as an assessment of
Freud the artist.

LEE, S. G. M. and HERBERT, MARTIN, eds. *Freud and Psychology.* Baltimore: Penguin Books, 1970. An important collection of essays on
Freud and psychological theory by B. A. Farrell, Arnold Bernstein
and others.

MARMOR, JUDD, ed. *Modern Psychoanalysis: New Directions and Perspectives*. New York: Basic Books, 1968. Essays reviewing psychoanalysis in light of current scientific investigation in many fields.

MASSERMAN, J. H., ed. *Psychoanalysis and Human Values*. New York: Grune and Stratton, 1960. An earlier collection of essays by Gardner Murphy and others.

PUMPIAN-MINDLIN, E., ed. *Psychoanalysis as Science*. Stanford: Stanford University Press, 1952. An even earlier collection concerned with problems of validation and definition.

SHERWOOD, MICHAEL. *The Logic of Explanation of Psychoanalysis*. New York: Academic Press, 1969. A critique of psychoanalytic scientific method.

WOLLHEIM, RICHARD. *Sigmund Freud*. New York: The Viking Press, 1971. A lucid and well-organized exposition of Freud's ideas as they evolved. A valuable discussion of the "Scientific Project" and its influence on Freud's later thinking.

III. Social Psychology and Philosophy

BAKAN, DAVID. *Sigmund Freud and the Jewish Mystical Tradition*. Princeton: D. Van Nostrand Company, 1958. Speculative but highly interesting inquiry into Freud's possible roots in Jewish mystical philosophy. A valuable discussion of *Moses and Monotheism*.

FROMM, ERICH. *The Crisis of Psychoanalysis*. New York: Holt Rinehart Winston, 1970. An important assessment of developments in psychoanalysis since Freud, with attention to ego psychology and the Freudian critique of society.

NELSON, BENJAMIN, ed. *Freud and the Twentieth Century*. New York: Meridian Books, 1957. Essays chiefly concerned with the cultural, philosophical and religious implications of psychoanalysis; by Herberg, Abraham Kaplan, Maritain, Niebuhr, Erikson, and others.

RICOEUR, PAUL. *Freud and Philosophy*. Translated by Denis Savage. New Haven: Yale University Press, 1970. Long, extremely technical but highly rewarding examination of Freud's philosophical assumptions and development of ideas. Indispensable.

RIEFF, PHILIP. *Freud: The Mind of the Moralist*. New York: Anchor Books, 1961. Not only one of the finest books ever written on Freud but a major cultural history, focusing on the social implications of Freud's thought. Also indispensable.

RIESMAN, DAVID. *Individualism Reconsidered*. New York: The Free Press, 1954. An assessment of Freud's theories of work, play, and religion, in four major essays.

ROAZEN, PAUL. *Freud: Political and Social Thought*. New York: Alfred A. Knopf, 1968. Freud's contributions to social and political thought, with attention to the problem of authority. Contains an important analysis of the study of Woodrow Wilson.

IV. Art and Literature

BURKE, KENNETH. *Language as Symbolic Action*. Berkeley: University of California Press, 1966. A theory of symbolic action in art based on Freud's "secondary thinking."

CREWS, FREDERICK, ed. *Psychoanalysis and Literary Process*. Cambridge, Mass.: Winthrop Publishers, 1970. A collection of essays by psychoanalytic critics. The introductory essay by Crews, "Anaesthetic Criticism," is one of the best defenses of psychoanalytic criticism ever written.

HOFFMAN, FREDERICK J. *Freudianism and the Literary Mind*. Second Edition. Baton Rouge: Lousiana State University Press, 1957. An early and valuable history of psychoanalytic criticism. A particularly valuable discussion of D. H. Lawrence.

HOLLAND, NORMAN. *The Dynamics of Literary Response*. New York: Oxford University Press, 1968. A major study of Freudian ideas and a "model" literary theory based on them. Indispensable.

———. *Psychoanalysis and Shakespeare*. New York: Oxford University Press, 1966. An exhaustive critique of psychoanalytic studies of Shakespeare.

HYMAN, STANLEY EDGAR. *The Tangled Bank: Darwin, Marx, Frazer and Freud as Imaginative Writers*. New York: Atheneum, 1962. Metaphorical patterns in Freud's writings.

LESSER, SIMON O. *Fiction and the Unconscious*. Boston: Beacon Press, 1957. Freudian ideas and their implications for literary theory. Indispensable.

MORRISON, CLAUDIA C. *Freud and the Critics: The Early Use of Depth Psychology in Literary Criticism*. Chapel Hill: University of North Carolina Press, 1968. Authoritative and useful. Important discussions of Conrad Aiken, Van Wyck Brooks, Lawrence.

PHILLIPS, WILLIAM, ed. *Art and Psychoanalysis*. New York: Meridian Books, 1963. A source book of essays chiefly concerned with art and neurosis, by Marie Bonaparte, Greenacre, Jones, Reik, Empson, Rank, Róheim, Fiedler, and Trilling among others.

RUITENBEEK, HENDRIK M., ed. *The Creative Imagination: Psychoanalysis and The Genius of Inspiration*. Chicago: Quadrangle Books, 1965. Essays by Klein, Rank, Rickman, Kris, Greenacre, Rollo May, and others on the psychoanalytic theory of creativity.

SCHAPIRO, MEYER. "Leonardo and Freud: An Art-Historical Study," *Journal of the History of Ideas*, 17 (1956), 147–78. A theoretical study of Freud's evidence in his study of Leonardo.

SLOCHOWER, HARRY. *Mythopoesis: Mythic Patterns in the Literary Classics*. Detroit: Wayne State University Press, 1970. Valuable use of Freud to analyze myths as they contribute to a single pattern in literature.

SPECTOR, JACK J. *The Aesthetics of Freud: A Study in Psychoanalysis and Art*. New York: Praeger, 1972. A comprehensive and authoritative review of background, theory, and influence.

WILSON, EDMUND. *The Wound and the Bow*. New York: Oxford University Press, 1947. The essay on Philoctetes remains one of the most important statements on art and neurosis.

Index

The works and theories of Freud are listed beneath his name.

DATE DUE			
AP 8 '82	MAR 29 '92		
DE 07 '84	DEC 6 '84		
MR 04 '85	MAR 1 '85		
AP 27 '86	APR 11 '86		
DE 08 '86	DEC 9 '86		
NO 09 '89	OCT 23 '89		
DE 01 '89	DEC 4 '89		
AP 03 '90	MAR 28 '90		